STOP THE
FIGHT!

AN ILLUSTRATED GUIDE FOR COUPLES

STOP THE FIGHT!

HOW TO BREAK FREE FROM
THE 12 MOST COMMON ARGUMENTS
AND BUILD A RELATIONSHIP THAT LASTS

MICHELLE BRODY, PhD

Vermilion
LONDON

10 9 8 7 6 5 4 3 2 1

Vermilion, an imprint of Ebury Publishing,
20 Vauxhall Bridge Road,
London SW1V 2SA

Vermilion is part of the Penguin Random House group of companies whose addresses can be found at
global.penguinrandomhouse.com

 Penguin
Random House
UK

First published in the United Kingdom by Vermilion in 2016
First published in the United States by The Experiment, LLC in 2015

www.eburypublishing.co.uk

A CIP catalogue record for this book is available from the British Library

ISBN 9781785040726

Printed and bound in Great Britain by Clays Ltd, St Ives PLC

Penguin Random House is committed to a sustainable future for our business, our readers and our planet.
This book is made from Forest Stewardship Council® certified paper.

To HAL

∞

CONTENTS

INTRODUCTION: *"Seeing" Your Way Out of Fights*   xi

1: *The Partner Improvement Fight*   1

2: *The Proving Your Point Fight*   17

3: *The Nagging-Tuning Out Fight*   29

4: *The Escalating Fight*   39

5: *The Household Responsibilities Fight*   55

6: *The Birthday Fight*   83

7: *The Bad Reputation Fight*   113

8: *The "You Don't Care About Me" Fight*   135

9: *The Parenting Differences Fight*   167

10: *The Money Fight*   187

11: *The Sex Fight*   221

12: *The Difficult Relatives Fight*   255

CONCLUSION: *The Big Picture*   285

Terms Used in *Stop the Fight!*   292

Acknowledgments   295

Index   299

About the Author   304

INTRODUCTION

"SEEING" YOUR WAY
OUT OF FIGHTS

COUPLES BICKER, ARGUE, AND FIGHT. It's part of the landscape of a relationship, just as much as the glorious passion of early love. Miserable couples fight of course, but happy couples do, too. Fights can sometimes lead to fantastic, loving resolutions, but they can also evolve into simmering resentment.

For many of us, there's nothing worse than the feeling you have after a frustrating fight with your partner. Imagine: You ask for a small favor, your partner overreacts, and the fight seems to explode out of nowhere, sending both of you into angry corners. Or, your partner criticizes you about something, and the crazy injustice of his or her complaint just makes you see red. After the fight, what stays in your memory are the awful things you said to one another, the amazement that you both just fought over something so ridiculous, and the real sense of hopelessness about whether the relationship is any good if you can have fights as nasty as that.

Sometimes fights seem to occur over the most foolish things, and looking back you can't imagine how you let yourself get so worked up about something so silly. It happens to all of us. I once went to a play that featured a scene with a middle-aged couple playing a game of cards. The husband made a comment about the game that the wife didn't like, and the wife responded in a snide tone of voice. The husband retorted something with a glare and the wife snarled back. Before our eyes, an innocent card game turned into a full-scale, throwing-dishes fight. The audience roared with laughter. Hilarious, that War of the Roses stuff—but only when you're not in the middle of it. From an outside perspective, it's easy to see how ridiculous it is for a single comment to ignite a long, painful battle, but underneath the audience's laughter is the stark recognition that we've all been there. The trivial becomes heartrending in astonishingly few exchanges.

And then the fights *repeat* themselves! How often do we find ourselves having the exact same fight that we had with our partner last week or last year about the exact same issue? Your partner said that annoying thing again, you reacted as you always do, and you're both back in the same frustrating pattern again, still with no way out. Or, maybe the fight gets going over a different issue, but your respective behaviors in the fight repeat themselves—you still shout at the top of your lungs and your partner still leaves the room, slamming the door on the way out.

After the fight, we think: How on earth will this ever change? We try all kinds of different methods—raising touchy subjects more gently, counting to ten to keep anger from boiling over, and trying to talk it over with one another—but nothing seems to work. We seek advice from books, magazines, or a therapist, and try to follow it, but sometimes, the changes we try make the fights worse. No wonder we give up! Let's face it: Relationship advice can be pretty dizzying in its complexity. Keeping track of the specific "right" and "wrong" things to say is challenging, especially once the fight actually begins and you can't remember any of it in the heat of the moment anyway.

We need a way to think about fights that's simple to understand and is easy to remember and put into practice. In my work as a couples coach, I've found that there's one thing above all that can help you stop repetitive fights, one thing that will help you regain control and start turning your interactions in a more positive direction.

To explore what that one thing is, let's return to the couple in the play I described earlier. Every time the wife felt hurt, she lashed out at her husband. Every time the husband felt insulted, he struck back at his wife. Each one was thoroughly convinced that he or she had been the innocent victim of the other's vicious attack and that the other person was completely, utterly wrong. They could each easily see how aggressive their partner was being, and they both felt their own pain, but only the audience could vividly see the suffering on both sides. The audience could see that neither partner was really right—while each was somewhat justified in his or her reaction, given the pain the other had caused, both also went too far, purposely pushing one another's buttons. Watching that fight, you could see that if they could just calm down enough to listen and straighten out the misunderstandings, they might have been able to save their china. If only they could see what it looked like from the outside! Unfortunately, in our own personal conflicts, it's hard to "get to the balcony" and see the fight from anywhere except from our own perspective, which prevents us from truly solving the problem at hand.

Achieving real change in couple interactions is about *seeing the big picture*. The moment you both understand why your fights start and how they escalate and become repetitive, is the moment you have an opening to change the pattern. What is "the balcony view" or "the big picture"? It is a large part of what couples pay for when they decide to seek professional help. The hope is that the therapist will have an objective perspective on the fight and will therefore be able to figure out how to solve it.

But what if you could do that without a therapist? When you and your partner can see that balcony view of your fight, in all of its complexity and from both sides, you can actually change the negative cycle yourselves. I've seen this amazing phenomenon over and over in my experience as a couples therapist. When a couple can visualize the dynamics at play in their fight, the fight settles down, the finger-pointing stops, and they each can take responsibility for what they've contributed and get more interested in understanding one another.

Stop the Fight! is a book that will help you see the big picture. In fact, it's a book full of pictures, with diagrams and illustrations that show you how to prevent and reverse the escalating conflicts in your relationship. Using simple drawings, I explain how disagreements become fights, why they stay fights, and how you can locate the keys to unraveling them. You'll get the "big picture" overview of some of the most common arguments between couples, and you'll also see, literally, ways you can stop the fight, alongside easy-to-remember illustrations of the tools and methods you can use to stop arguments from repeating themselves.

My goal is to provide a quick way to get the conversation going between you and your partner. Couples can look at each image in this book and ask: "Is this what's going on between us? Is this how it looks from your side? Can we both agree to try this strategy?" You can discuss it together, point out where it captures or does not capture the specifics of your unique fight, and test what happens when, together, you look at the problem from a different angle. Change starts with thinking about the problem in a new light.

As you read through the chapters of this book, you'll notice that many of the concepts interrelate. Some might even seem to be different ways to say the same thing. In the realm of relationships and couples, it's true that there are many paths to the opportunity for change. I've found in my practice that ideas resonate differently with every couple, so in this book I try to share a variety of approaches that provided an "Aha!" moment for the couples I've worked with.

I hope that you and your partner will find an "Aha!" in the following pages to help you open the door to solving your fight.

In this book, I make the point that, in some ways, all couples fight the same fights. Gay or straight, male or female, we can all find ourselves on one side or another of the fights portrayed here. Indeed, the chapters are called The Money Fight, The Nagging-Tuning Out Fight, The Parenting Differences Fight, and so on, which reflects my view that when we have these fights there are some very common underlying dynamics at play. However, even though there are many similarities, there are important nuances that make each individual couple's fights unique. Your version of The Sex Fight or any other fight may be quite different than the examples I use. My hope, however, is that despite the specific differences in your relationship you can gain some overall insight for stopping the fight.

A final caveat: While this book can help couples alter their interactions with one another, conflicts in relationships can be quite complex, and there's no easy fix for situations that have been destructive for many years. This book can help couples in entrenched fights to understand and lower the intensity of their fights, which can give you the opportunity to then rebuild the connection that became so damaged by the battles. But fights can also leave deep emotional wounds that are hard to heal without professional help. If you're struggling with your partner in a pattern of fights that feels insurmountable, don't put off trying couples therapy. I frequently see couples who wish they'd come in ten years earlier—their relationship was suffering terribly, but it was hard for them to imagine there was a way to fix it. Years go by and the fights grow worse, or they go underground. There have been great strides in research on therapies for couples, with better and better outcomes. There's no better time than now for you and your partner to stop the fight.

CHAPTER 1

THE PARTNER IMPROVEMENT FiGHT

AT THE BEGINNING OF **A** new relationship, everything feels like sunshine and roses.

Inevitably, though, two people spending a lot of time with one another begin to notice that they have differences. Some dissatisfaction creeps in.

Over time, if that small annoying quality doesn't change, frustration and tension grow.

When your partner acts in a way that upsets, worries, or disappoints you, you may naturally feel the urge to change it, often by saying something to your partner.

Why don't you just tell your brother?

What kind of person does that?

Can you give me some space?

Please don't interrupt me.

I've never seen someone as spoiled as you.

If you do that again, I will leave.

Why don't you ever initiate sex?

You have to call me if you're running late!

You are wasting your time doing that.

You don't pay enough attention to me, all you do is play online games.

I've told you that really bothers me. Why have you done it again?

You need to be more careful with money.

Stop shouting at me!

Please try to be neater.

You can't make plans with your family on weekends!

It's usually a good idea to gas up the car before you get home.

If you drink like that again, I won't sleep with you for a month.

Some things you try to change are "small annoying things," like how your partner folds laundry, but there are also those big, difficult things that put the relationship or your lifestyle at risk, like differences in spending, attention, sex, or parenting. Partners use whatever strategies they can to try to change the problem they see in front of them. Gentle reminders, direct requests, helpful advice, complaining, or threats—all of these tools we use for Partner Improvement.

KIND REQUESTS

Can you give me some space?

Please don't interrupt me.

Please try to be neater.

TEACHABLE MOMENTS, SUGGESTIONS, & ADVICE

It's usually a good idea to gas up the car before you get home.

You need to be more careful with money.

Why don't you just tell your brother?

COMPLAINTS

Why don't you ever initiate sex?

You don't pay enough attention to me; all you do is play online games.

I've told you that really bothers me. Why have you done it again?

DEMANDS

Stop shouting at me!

You can't make plans with your family on weekends!

You have to call me if you're running late!

THREATS

If you do that again, I will leave.

If you don't stop spending I will open a separate bank account.

If you drink like that again, I won't sleep with you for a month.

OUTRIGHT CRITICISM

You are wasting your time doing that.

What kind of person does that?

I've never seen someone as spoiled as you.

Certain methods clearly work better than others. As we all know, and as many communication experts remind us, kindness or helpful suggestions usually achieve better results than demands, criticism, or threats.

But sometimes, what we think of as a helpful suggestion brings surprising resistance from our partner. They don't listen or change what they're doing, and they may even get angry, and start a fight. What a frustrating mystery! Why don't our Partner Improvement efforts work, and why do they sometimes just ignite fights?

Let's look at Mike and Mary Jo's situation as an example. Mary Jo is starting to get nervous about how much time Mike spends playing games online, and Mike is beginning to stress out about Mary Jo's shopping habits. Here, Mike tries to engage in some Partner Improvement:

> You are really spending more than we can afford. You don't know how to control yourself. You're going to make us lose our house.

Whoa, Mary Jo does not look happy! She storms off and refuses to talk to Mike about it anymore, Mike walks away, feeling even more demoralized—not only is Mary Jo's spending a problem, but he experiences what a lot of people feel after a Partner Improvement effort: "Trying to talk about it makes it worse!"

So what went wrong?

Partner Improvement is tricky business. Even though you might have the best intentions when you ask your partner to change, your partner is likely to only hear a shadow of negative subtext underneath what you say:

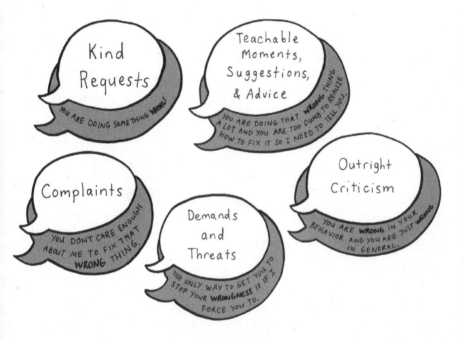

We human beings do not like to be told we're wrong and are very attuned to feeling personally attacked. So even when we don't intend to suggest that our partner is wrong, that's often the message that's heard. He or she is wrong for spending money, wrong for playing video games, wrong for speaking in that manner, or wrong in general for living the way he or she does. We all want acceptance, to be loved the way we are, so feeling judgment from our partner, real or perceived, sticks out like a little barb. Some people are more sensitive to judgment than others, but barbs from a person with whom you're intimately connected usually hurt.

Think about it. You've chosen a partner because at some point or another, you thought highly of that person. You respected him or her, and respected his or her values and opinions. To hear, then, this same person criticizing you is a deep blow. After all, you yourself value (or valued) your partner's perspective, so their negative opinion of you carries a lot of weight, even if you'd rather not admit that to yourself.

Mike didn't realize that what he said to Mary Jo came across as if he had thrown darts at her:

Because Mary Jo heard only the shadow subtext of "wrong" and felt the arrows of Mike's attack, she wasn't open to listening to what Mike was requesting and instead felt defensive and closed to his feedback. Mike's message not only didn't get through, it inadvertently touched off a fight. Mary Jo also detected a subtext of a characterization of herself that felt insulting: that she's a person who is out of control and capable of causing disaster. She doesn't see herself that way, and she feels stung when she hears that Mike might think of her that way.

STOPPING THE PARTNER IMPROVEMENT FIGHT: REMOVE THE JUDGMENT

One key to stopping the Partner Improvement Fight is to remove any and all implications of judgment from what you're trying to say. In fact, go one step further and try to remove the judgment from your thoughts, too. (More on that in The Difficult Relatives Fight.)

Let's see what happens when Mike gives the conversation another try. This time, he goes into it with a mindset of love and concern for Mary Jo and makes sure not to show judgment for her shopping. Here's what he might say:

By stating his predicament in this manner, Mike communicates to Mary Jo that he doesn't want to interfere with her happiness or be critical of something she loves to do. He also gives her the benefit of the doubt and asks her to help with something he's worried about. In all of these ways, Mike invites Mary Jo to generously help him with his anxiety rather than criticizing her or blaming her for causing it.

Removing judgment from your message is the basis of almost all communication advice. Notice how the common suggestions of good relationship communication all involve some version of removing judgment from what you say to a partner.

TYPICAL COMMUNICATION ADVICE	HOW IT HELPS	REMOVES JUDGMENT?
Use "I" statements"	You are expressing your own feelings rather than judging (or blaming) the other person by saying, "you did this or that"	✔
Put yourself in your partner's shoes	You understand the other person's motives and see him or her as reasonable, so you're less judgmental	✔
Ask questions to understand	You learn more about the other person's feelings, which allows you to adopt a less critical view of his or her situation	✔
Focus on appreciation	You notice what your partner does that is positive instead of actions you're inclined to judge	✔

FEEDBACK WITHOUT JUDGMENT

While it's human nature to dislike being judged by others, we're also hardwired to want to learn and grow, at least when we have good motivation to do so. And partners who help each other grow will strengthen their bond with each other. So how can you help your partner learn without landing in the Partner Improvement Fight? It's all in how you offer your feedback.

Feedback served on a platter of true caring and consideration is palatable; feedback served with judgment and criticism turns your stomach.

When you offer feedback with love and concern and truly extract any critiques or disdain, your partner will hear it a whole lot better. If you keep judgment out of your relationship in general, you'll build trust. If your partner knows that he or she can always trust that your requests are coming from a place of love and are without judgment, he or she will want to pay attention to your suggestions and consider making a behavior adjustment.

"JUST CHANGE AND THERE'S NO FIGHT!"

Maybe you're thinking that there wouldn't have been a fight at all if Mary Jo had just listened to Mike and changed her spending habits. Sure, she could have. But if Mary Jo did what Mike asked yet simultaneously felt criticized, the problem wouldn't go away. Resentment could build under the surface and lead to other fights down the road. On the other hand, if Mike shares his feedback without judgment, Mary Jo will be open to listening and therefore able to change her habits without resentment.

IS ADVICE A WAY TO HELP OR A WAY TO DISTANCE?

Sometimes offering advice to your partner can be a great gift that truly helps. If your partner is in a fix and unsure of what to do, your advice can give them a way out of his or her trouble and provide relief.

But all too frequently, unsolicited advice will ignite a fight and cause trouble in couple relationships. Here's why: Advice-givers often have excellent intentions—all they want to do is to help—but the act of giving feedback can, paradoxically, create a wedge of distance between partners. In a subtle way, offering advice separates the two partners into the "teacher" and the "learner"—the one who has the advice to give, and the one who needs advice. A teacher-learner relationship is a bit more distant, a bit more unequal than a balanced relationship between intimate partners, and when the interaction veers toward a teacher-learner dynamic in a couple's relationship, people can usually feel the shift.

In this case, there doesn't seem to be any obvious judgment in the husband's advice. He genuinely wants to make his wife's life less stressful. But that subtle shift to advising or teaching makes his wife feel slightly more alone in the problem.

Instead of handing out unsolicited advice, sitting together in the soup of your partner's stress closes the distance between the two of you. The relief of not being alone in the struggle gives your partner the extra support he or she needs, which might be a game-changer in solving the problem on his or her own.

Another way to think about it is like this:

Offering advice focuses on the *problem* she faces, not on the *pain* in her face. When he gets really interested in the problem she's carrying, with all of its complexity, and thinks about potential solutions, it can actually distract his attention from the fact that there's a person struggling under that problem. She senses his greater interest in the problem than in her and feels the distance between them that it creates; therefore the advice he genuinely proposes inadvertently increases her pain.

Here he sees beyond the problem, and his attention is directed to the fact that *she* is struggling. When he discusses what he sees about *her*, she instantly perceives that she has a partner in the pain and feels closer to him, making it easier to either to solve the problem on her own or accept his help in solving it. It's not about carrying the problem box for the other person—it's about seeing just how hard it is to carry it.

THE PARTNER IMPROVEMENT FIGHT TOOLBOX

 Recognize that your Partner Improvement efforts might be conveying judgment about your partner.

 Remove any judgment. Try showing concern, collaborating, and giving your partner the benefit of the doubt.

 When responding to a partner's problem, offer empathy to build connection.

 Focus on your partner, not on the problem.

CHAPTER 2

THE
PROVING YOUR POINT
FIGHT

LIKE MOST MATTERS REGARDING COUPLES, there are two sides to every story.

Charles's side looks like this:

Charles comes into my office and describes the scene: "I come home from my incredibly stressful job and I really want there to be a calm environment at home. I tell Teresa that I wish I could have about thirty minutes at home to decompress before I jump in to help with the kids. She instantly gets furious at me and complains about her day and everything she's had to do. So there I am . . . walking in to complaining, chaos—there's toys everywhere, the TV is blaring, the kids are wild—and no one even says hello to me."

Teresa can hardly sit still as he spends a few minutes proving his point. Teresa's side looks like this:

She tells me, "We agreed that it made sense for me to quit my full-time job when we started a family and do consulting work from home while being there for the children. I work really hard to take care of what needs to get done on the home front. I deal with the kids all day and I don't care what anyone says, it's more exhausting and stressful than sitting in an office like he does. He even gets dinner made for him! I don't have that privilege. It's just excruciating for me to hear him claim that *he* needs calm and that it's like a tornado when he gets home. How can he possibly be so blind!? The kids have done their homework, the baby is bathed, our son is practicing his music, I've run errands and cooked, and I haven't had a second to myself all day to make a work call!"

Charles throws up his hands. "That's just not reality!"

The couple continues the battle for who is correct in their assessment of the situation.

What is the truth? Is the house a non-relaxing mess to come home to, or is it the product of much effort to prepare for dinner and family time? Clearly, Charles and Teresa each see the scene through the lens of their own experience. But when they present their view of the situation to one another, the gulf between the two "truths" is tremendous, and the fight moves to proving whose truth is correct.

They each gather evidence to make a convincing case for their point of view. They each insist that they're right and the other is clearly wrong.

The fight continues, with both partners trying more and more strenuously to win the argument. The more they try to prove their own point, the more the fight heats up. But as with any fight that's essentially about "being right," there's an important problem: Proving Your Point Fights, or Right–Wrong Fights, never resolve themselves. Here's the Big Picture View of Right–Wrong Fights:

1. Right-Wrong Fights get stuck. The more you insist that your view is right, the more your partner tells you that you're wrong, and vice versa, so nothing changes with each round of the fight except increasing aggravation.

2. Convincing arguments don't convince. In Right–Wrong Fights neither partner can convince the other that their position is correct. Consider that there are two possible outcomes of a Right–Wrong Fight, and both are unlikely to happen:

Outcome 1: I convince my partner that I'm right and then my partner realizes he or she is wrong and therefore gives up his or her position. This outcome doesn't happen because my partner is unlikely to suddenly accept that he or she has been wrong all along, especially in the heat of a fight.

Outcome 2: My partner convinces me that I'm wrong and he or she is right, and I give up my position. This outcome doesn't happen because I won't give in when I *know* I'm in the right.

In the example of Charles and Teresa, Charles hopes that Teresa will give up her view that the house is in good shape and come to agree with him that the house is in chaos. Teresa hopes that Charles will see that she's right and that she does a great job managing to get everything orderly by dinner, and will recognize his error in thinking there's a problem.

Both of these outcomes are unlikely because they imply a winner and a loser, and no one wants to be that loser. In a Proving Your Point Fight, both partners work hard to convince the other of the rightness of their own side and the wrongness of their partner's side. Neither side is open to being convinced, so the fight won't end unless one person capitulates because he or she can't stand to continue fighting. Or, sometimes someone proposes to "just agree to disagree" to try to end the fight without a winner. But that doesn't truly settle it either.

Proving Your Point Fights about specific, provable issues (such as who correctly remembers which weekend we last visited your mother) can get heated, but ultimately, there's a fact that can be hunted down to break the tie. But like Charles and Teresa's fight, many Proving Your Point Fights are simply the same scene viewed from two different perspectives, seen through the lenses of two distinct sets of feelings and experiences. In the case of Charles and Teresa, the battle is about much more than how the house looks, and therefore "agreeing to disagree" doesn't help them. For both partners something bigger is at stake, which makes neither one willing to give in. Uncovering what's really at stake in the fight opens the door to solving it.

STOPPING THE PROVING YOUR POINT FIGHT

The contradiction between Teresa's and Charles's truths can be reconciled if they understand *why* they're each trying so hard to prove that their view is right. After Charles comes home at the end of a long day, he's deeply in need of a moment of comfort and rest. When walking into the house doesn't make him feel like he had hoped, he's frustrated and wants the situation to change. So he tries to describe to Teresa what he experiences when he gets home: too much chaos. He wants to help her understand how desperately he needs it to be different.

When Teresa appears to refuse to acknowledge the chaos that feels so obvious to him, Charles pushes his point harder, pointing out everything that isn't orderly. He may not be totally conscious of it, but his need for rest drives his side of the Proving Your Point Fight; his peace of mind is at stake.

Teresa hears Charles's criticism of the house and can't believe he doesn't see what's plainly obvious to her: that the house

in is great shape, given all she juggled today. With tending to the kids, preparing meals, and doing household chores, her experience is that she has been cleaning up chaos all day long! It's outrageous to her that Charles won't acknowledge how much she's done and in fact, only notices what isn't perfect. By describing everything in the house that looks good and runs smoothly, she tries to get him to see what he's apparently ignoring—all her hard work.

When Charles seems to refuse to acknowledge her efforts, Teresa pushes her point even harder. In the moment, she may not know exactly why it's so critical that she prove Charles wrong, but her root desire for some acknowledgment drives Teresa's side of the Proving Your Point Fight.

Here's another way to think about it: When Charles says he wants calm at home, his *intent* is to express his wish for relief from his stress and to ask for Teresa's help in attaining that. His intention is good, but his impact lands badly—it falls on Teresa as a criticism.

In her response, Teresa's *intent* is to ask Charles to at least notice all the hard work she puts into running the household everyday. Her intention is also good, but it too has a bad impact—Charles hears it as a denial of his reality and the need he just expressed. In the end, she feels criticized and he feels unheard.

Looking at this fight from the Big Picture View, you can see that a terrible misunderstanding is going on in both directions. So how can that be stopped? The first step is to take a different view of your partner's action and see that:

IMPACT ≠ INTENT

Separating intent from impact allows Charles and Teresa to recognize that *unintentional* bad impacts are causing all the trouble. They both have good intentions that are justified and reasonable, but they're also responsible for the bad impact their words have on one another.

In this kind of fight, partners are often able to easily talk about their own good intent and their partner's bad impact. And they're both "right"—they *do* have good intent, and their partner's action *does* have bad impact.

> You had such a **BAD IMPACT** on me! And I only had **GOOD INTENTION** that you missed!

Doing the opposite is much harder but much more useful. Focusing on your own bad impact and recognizing your partner's good intent does a lot to stop the fight.

> I see the **BAD IMPACT** I had on you. And I see you only had **GOOD INTENTIONS**.

This little twist accomplishes a few important things that help to end an argument. First, you each *take responsibility* for hurting one another. You also acknowledge that your partner's impact was *unintentional* and not purposely hurtful. Last, you shift your focus to consider what everyone's *true intentions* are, acknowledging that you're both good people trying to solve something that matters to you a lot.

HOW TO SAY IT

I know you intended

_____ ... but

GOOD INTENTION

here's how it hit me ...

_____ .

UNFORTUNATE BAD IMPACT

Discussing intent and impact using this kind of approach communicates to your partner that you still see him or her as a good person with reasonable intentions ("I know you intended . . . "), but it also helps him or her to understand that it impacted you badly, which was likely not your partner's intention (" . . . but unfortunately, it hit me. . . .").

Here's how Teresa and Charles ended up stopping their fight:

Can we talk about what happened yesterday? I realize now that when I said I need calm, when I get home, **THAT MADE YOU FEEL INSULTED,** like I don't notice all you do here at the house. Is that right?

Thank you for coming back to it. Yeah, that is what I felt. It kills to hear you say it's not calm when you come home because I fight the chaos all day and it's calmer because of it when you get home.

I can only imagine the chaos you deal with. I do really appreciate what you do. Can you understand what it feels like for me, though?

I guess I can. It's hard for me not to think you have the easier deal. **BUT I CAN SEE THAT YOU JUST WANT SOME PEACE AT THE END OF YOUR DAY.** How can we work it out that you and I get the break we need at that crazy hour?

Notice that after Charles acknowledges that he's had a bad impact on Teresa, she's better able to see his good intent. And once they both recognize what the other actually intended, they have a much better chance of helping one another with the real and important needs that underlie their need to prove a point.

THE PROVING YOUR POINT FIGHT TOOLBOX

 Recognize when your fight has turned into a Proving Your Point or Right–Wrong Fight and acknowledge that you won't be able to change one another's minds.

 Uncover what's at stake for you and your partner in proving that you're right.

 Recognize that while you have good intentions, the way you are expressing them may still have a bad impact on your partner.

 Talk with your partner with your focus on your bad impact and his or her good intentions.

IMPACT ≠ INTENT

CHAPTER 3

THE NAGGING-TUNING OUT FIGHT

LEFT UNRESOLVED, THE PARTNER IMPROVEMENT Fight can morph into the Nagging-Tuning Out Fight. When we don't see the change we had hoped for from our Partner Improvement attempt, we often try again using a different tactic. If you patiently explained the problem before, you might say it more emphatically this time, and the next time, you'll loudly complain or demand a change. Pretty quickly, your efforts start to look like nagging.

Let's look at it from the other person's perspective. Feeling nagged typically makes a person want to tune out and ignore the nagger's advice or request or take some space. But, if you keep disengaging, it's hard to get back to communicating in a positive way. A couple stuck in the Nagging-Tuning Out Fight feels "we just can't communicate anymore," or "everything starts a fight." Julie and Nigel are one such couple.

Here's how Julie describes Nigel:

To help, Julie calls from the office to remind Nigel to work on his résumé. Nigel is at home, composing cover letters, calling potential contacts, and trying to make progress on his job hunt. When Julie phones, he feels more demoralized than he was before and decides to take a snack break.

Nigel wishes Julie would show more positive support, so when she gets home he tries to explain some of his struggles to her—the tough cold calls that led nowhere and the terrible job market in his field. He hopes she'll say something that will make tomorrow easier. But, when Julie hears about his day, she immediately begins to worry that nothing is changing and wonders if he's trying hard enough and actually taking the necessary steps. Wanting to be helpful, she makes some suggestions or tells him of another idea she heard about that might help him in his job hunt. But, all those suggestions make Nigel feel more alone in his job trouble. So he tells Julie that if she'd just stop nagging him, he'd get a job sooner. And he resolves not to talk to her about what he does all day so she can't nag him. After a few days of this, Julie takes his silence to mean he's doing even less than before.

Nigel and Julie each see themselves as the victim of the other's actions. It's the other person who is doing something wrong or bad. In Julie's eyes, Nigel is wrong because he's being passive in his job search. In Nigel's eyes, Julie is wrong because she's nagging him about something he's trying his best to change.

They both endure bad impacts from one another's words and actions. But, when they try to do something to fix the situation, they feel like they hit a brick wall. Every time Julie tries to get Nigel to take more action, he seems to resist changing and becomes even more passive! And no matter what Nigel does to try to get Julie to stop nagging, it only seems to bring on more negativity from her.

If you view the fight in this linear manner, the brick walls look impenetrable and the argument appears to be unsolvable. Nothing that Nigel and Julie do to try to change one another's behavior works. It becomes hard to find any hope that suddenly something will change when they've each hit that brick wall so many times. Fortunately, there's a way out. It starts with seeing that the fight is actually circular, not linear.

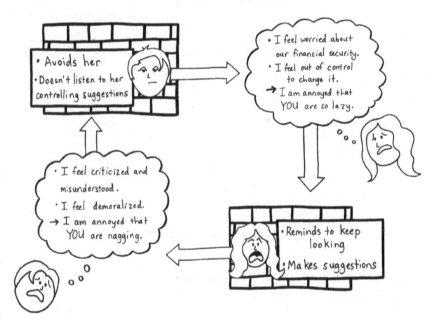

Each partner's actions seem justified given the frustrating behavior that they've noticed in the other person. Take Julie, for example. Who wouldn't try to help a partner who's struggling with a job hunt? Offering suggestions and trying to make sure Nigel stays on top of the task is certainly logical behavior that comes from a positive motivation to help. As for Nigel, it's understandable that he might have trouble finding a job, occasionally get demoralized, and therefore sometimes slow down in his efforts, especially if he feels controlled and prodded by Julie.

Both behaviors are reasonable given what each partner feels, but the actions and words they choose to convey those feelings don't come across as reasonable to their partner. Julie focuses on how Nigel's slowdown hurts her, and she starts to judge him. Nigel focuses on how Julie's reminders hurt him, and he starts to resent her. That judgment and resentment lead them to exhibit *more* of the behaviors that bother the other. It becomes the proverbial vicious cycle. Couples often describe fights as "going around in circles," which is a very accurate description of what's happening.

Here's the underlying structure of fights like this:

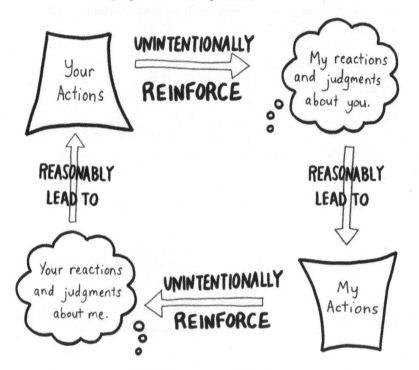

Fights that persist and repeat almost always follow a pattern like this. They are most definitely circular, not linear. A linear fight would suggest that one person is, without question, doing something wrong to the other and needs to change to make the fight stop. Circular fights have *two* parties that contribute to keep it going. Both partners are doing something that perpetuates the fight and makes it grow worse over time. Nigel or Julie might want to say, "I'm not even partially to blame for this fight that's happening between us!" But that's not really true—even if they mean well, even if they have good intentions, they *unintentionally* hurt one another. They're each trying to solve the problem they see in front of them in the way that makes the most sense to them personally. Unfortunately, the actions that come with their good intentions have a problematic impact on the other partner. Fortunately, recognizing that their fight is circular gives them options to resolve it.

STOPPING THE NAGGING-TUNING OUT FIGHT

Once you see that you're caught in a fight cycle, it's clear that you have to do something *different* to break free from it. Continuing the same actions just continues to drive the cycle. The tools for stopping a circular fight apply not only to the Nagging-Tuning Out Fight, but to all circular relationship fights as you will see in other chapters.

HOW AM I CONTRIBUTING?

To break free from the cycle of conflict, first focus on your *own* actions, not your partner's. Ask yourself, "Is there anything *I* might be doing that contributes to this fight I'm having with my partner?" When Julie really thought about it, she realized that calling from her job to remind Nigel to work on his résumé didn't seem to be making him any more motivated. Her reminders weren't helping and, more importantly, she could see that they were demoralizing to Nigel. For his part, Nigel realized that still wearing pajamas when Julie got home was not a neutral thing—it was actively agitating to Julie. The demoralization and agitation then triggered more passivity and nagging. Both partners recognized that some of their actions contributed to the circular fight they were caught in. This was a start. But they also needed to see that their cycle isn't just driven by their actions.

IT'S THE THOUGHTS THAT COUNT

The key to breaking free from the vicious cycle is found in the thought bubbles.

My reactions and judgments about you

When words or actions generate a strong reaction in a person, especially during a fight, judgment often follows. And as we saw in the first chapter, judgment brings trouble.

The judgement is happening in both directions. Julie reacts to Nigel's slow action on his job hunt: It worries her and makes her feel out of control. Then she forms a judgment about his behavior: He's lazy. That judgment drives her to try to *make* Nigel stop being lazy, and she decides to do that by reminding, or in his view, nagging him. Julie's judgment seeps through in her words and actions and Nigel perceives that. As a result, Julie's behavior doesn't seem at all reasonable or positive to him: "She isn't making suggestions or offering advice because she supports me. No, she's doing it because she thinks I'm not capable of thinking of it myself. Or, she thinks she has to micromanage me like I'm a kid!" He feels judged, and the distance between them grows as Julie's advice makes her come across more as a teacher or parent to Nigel than as an equal partner in their relationship.

- I feel worried about our financial security.
- I feel out of control to change it.
→ I am annoyed that YOU are so lazy.

But Nigel has his own judgments of Julie, too: Nigel's reaction to Julie's feedback is to feel criticized, misunderstood, and hurt. His pain turns into a judgment of Julie as nagging and controlling. Julie begins to sense that he thinks of her in this way. That, in turn, prevents her from viewing his lack of progress with compassion: "He can't blame his laziness on me . . . I'm only trying to help! This is so unfair to me!"

To stop this fight, Nigel and Julie each need to take a look at how they're contributing to the fight cycle with their *thoughts* about one another and the way they judge the other's behavior. So how do you *not judge* your partner? One way is to change your focus from your personal feelings regarding your good intentions and your partner's bad impact, to recognize the other side of the situation, and realize your own bad impact and your partner's good intent.

- I feel criticized and misunderstood.
- I feel demoralized.
→ I am annoyed that YOU are nagging.

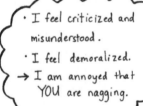

IMPACT ≠ INTENT

Nigel doesn't *intend* to work slowly on his job hunt—he absolutely wants to get a job. But sometimes, despite his good intentions, the pressure gets to him and he needs to take a break. Unfortunately, taking that break has a bad impact on his relationship by adding to Julie's worry.

Julie doesn't *intend* to nag Nigel—she's all about trying to help him. But sometimes, despite her good intentions, she becomes nervous and feels she has to say something to him. This, of course, has a bad impact on Nigel. If you are or ever were in the position of Julie or Nigel, you can easily see their underlying good intent—of the side you're familiar with! The challenge is seeing that *your partner* is acting with good intentions, even if all you feel is the bad impact.

RECOGNIZE THE CYCLE

The tools of the previous chapters apply to the Nagging-Tuning Out Fight. Keeping judgment out of your suggestions to your partner helps to get your message heard. And separating your partner's intent from his or her impact allows you to see beyond the behavior you don't like. But most importantly, acknowledging that your fight is circular entirely changes how the two of you view why you're stuck. Notice that this fight is not just "The Nagging Fight" or "The Tuning Out Fight." The nagging *and* the tuning out both contribute to the painful, unrelenting cycle that the two partners enact together. *Both* partners inadvertently keep the fight going. And since both of you are contributing, consider how you're contributing—in your actions, words, and judgments of one another. Once you recognize it, you can begin to talk about *the cycle* as the problem, without blaming one another: "We're getting stuck in that cycle again, where I get frustrated when it seems like you're not taking enough action, and then I end up nagging you, which makes you want to distance yourself from me even more. I don't want to do that to you, and I don't want to feel helpless either. Let's break out of this cycle."

How you make the changes to stop the fight cycle is what the rest of this book is about. But first, we consider a difficult problem. Sometimes, before you have a chance to stop a circular fight, it takes a turn for the worse, escalating beyond what you ever imagined when the fight started.

THE NAGGING-TUNING OUT FIGHT TOOLBOX

 Recognize that "unsolvable fights" are usually circular.

 In circular fights, *both* partners' actions drive the cycle of conflict, even if one partner seems louder than the other.

Stopping the fight cycle is a joint commitment—both partners have to change how they contribute to the cycle.

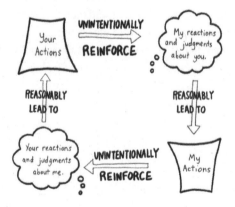

CHAPTER 4

THE
ESCALATING
FIGHT

"**H**EY, WHY DID YOU CHANGE the channel?"

"I want to see the game."

"So go check the score online—I'm watching a show."

"I know the score; I want to see the game."

"Well, I was watching my show first! Go watch in the kitchen."

"I don't want to watch in the kitchen; I want to sit on the couch. Why do you have to watch that dumb show anyway?"

"It's not dumb. I had a hard day today at work and I'm relaxing here and you just come along and think you can change the channel. NO."

"Oh, great. Now you're going to remind me 'how hard you work' for the millionth time."

"Damn right I do. And you never appreciate what I do for this family!"

"You're always begging for people to fawn all over you and thank you for having a job. You aren't the only one around here working! I'm tired, too, and I want to watch the game!"

"Yeah, right. I bet you're *real* tired from meeting with your *one* customer today."

"You know very well that business is slow. That's just mean."

"I just think you don't know what it means to work hard. You always think you're doing so much, but you have no idea what I go through in a day. The crap I have to deal with in my department, my crazy boss, and then I come home and all I want is a little peace to watch my show but *no*, you can't even give me that. Do I have to do literally everything around here?"

"What's that supposed to mean? You're constantly complaining about everything. I've to always listen to you rant on and on. If you hate your job so much why don't you just quit already?!"

"You know very well that I can't quit. If you could man up and actually provide for this family I'd finally be able to!!"

"Oh yeah? You know what? You're even crazier than your witch of a mother! I can't stand being around you. I'm outta here!"

When a fight ends like this, with someone leaving the room or some other dramatic explosion, both partners can feel a bit shell-shocked. What the heck happened there? What happened to discussing what to watch on TV? How did it turn into a fight about crazy mothers and providing for the family? How did it get so big so fast? And how can you stop a fight like this?

An escalating fight can seem like it's barreling down a train track with no brakes. It feels like it can't be stopped until it runs out of track and crashes. But unlike a runaway train, Escalating Fights are somewhat predictable in the pattern that they follow. Seeing that pattern can help you stop them.

By their very nature, Escalating Fights progress from stings to darts to rubber bullets to live ammo to cannons, and as soon as you take up a stronger weapon, your partner will aim a stronger one, too. If you both keep going, eventually you create a mushroom cloud.

The key to preventing mutual destruction is the same as it would be in a global nuclear arms race: As a computer in the 1980s movie, *War Games,* wisely concludes, "The only winning move is not to play."

No matter the root of the fight, escalation has some common steps, and each one uses a particular type of weaponry. Both partners have ammunition available to them, which they can and will choose to use if provoked to rise to a higher level of intensity. This ammunition can be considered in three categories of power:

Current Arrows: These are facts about the current situation, which you deploy to try to prove that you're right and deserve to win this fight. In the fight over the television, current arrows may include:

* "You got to watch what you wanted last night, so I should be able to choose tonight!"
* "I was here first."
* "I'm tired; why can't you cut me some slack?"

If logical pleas don't bring about a win, partners will often throw in a barbed arrow about the current situation, offering an insult instead of a justification to try to quickly push the other person to give in. Calling the show "dumb" or pointing out how *you* had a "hard day at work" are arrows that will cause the stung partner to reach for the next level of weaponry.

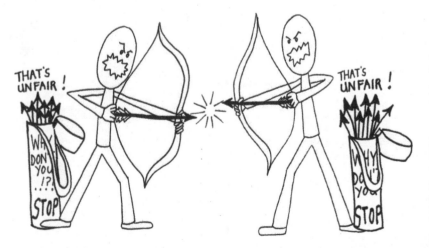

Historical Bombs: These are stories from the past, experiences from earlier in your relationship that left you with feelings of unfairness or pain that you haven't yet let go. While at war with your partner, you reach into your arsenal of "historical bombs" to strengthen your case in the fight at hand:

* "Remember when you asked me to do you that big favor? I did it. When was the last time you did me a big favor? You should do what I want for once!"
* "You complained so much on that vacation! You were completely out of control—just like you are now!"
* "Don't you remember how you messed up that evening by getting home so late? That's just another example of how inconsiderate you are!"

People often pull out stories like these to bolster their argument, and let's face it: There are few things more annoying than your partner bringing up that old, stupid incident yet again. But once your partner mentions it, you reach back into your own chest of stories and raise counterarguments that are equally hurtful.

Weapons of Mass Destruction (WMD): These are the truly nasty things you could say that would hurt your partner most because they strike at his or her deepest vulnerabilities. You know that saying these things would seriously cross a line. In essence, using a WMD during a fight turns something your partner trusted telling you about themselves into a weapon against them.

Intimate partners tend to have plenty of WMDs in their arsenals because they know one another well enough to know what is most hurtful. For example, if your partner has revealed to you his painful memories of his mother using profanity to demean him, shouting profanities at the height of a fight would be deploying a WMD. If you know your partner has deep fears of abandonment, it would be launching a laser-guided WMD to storm out of the house and threaten to never return.

A disagreement about something small, like which TV show to watch, can escalate quickly if one party pulls out a stronger weapon. In the fight at the beginning of this chapter, the first escalation happens as the man calls the woman's show "dumb." In some couples, deriding the other person's TV choices doesn't cross a line of insult; for those couples, banter about TV choices is tolerated. But, for the couple in this example, and for many others, the first hint of an insult about something one of them likes is perceived as an insult about who that person is.

She counters his insult by explaining why watching the show right now is important to her, but she also slips in the comment, "I had a hard day at work," which he recognizes as a comparison and therefore finds insulting. He then pulls out a story from his past experience, deflecting her implied jab about his work by mocking how predictable she is with her complaining.

The two proceed to exchange stories from their history:

* ✳ "You always. . . . "
* ✳ "You never. . . . "
* ✳ "You just don't know. . . ."
* ✳ "You can't even give me that!"

Eventually, they progress to the Weapons of Mass Destruction: deep personal attacks that hit the most vulnerable nerves. She knows that he's truly pained that she makes more money than he does, and the "man up" comment lands a particularly cruel blow on that vulnerability. However, as in nuclear war, once one warhead has been launched, the other side retaliates. In this case, he fires back by intentionally provoking deeply painful feelings about her mother.

In the heat of the battle, we don't recognize that every one of our negative actions makes the whole encounter worse for both parties. Each partner acts with an "I don't care if we both lose, as long as you don't win" mindset. Letting the other person have the last word or last shot feels like defeat, so the retaliation continues.

STOPPING THE ESCALATING FIGHT

The best way to avoid a nuclear showdown in your relationship is to prevent it through restraint—by agreeing not to play that dangerous war game. Ideally, before any escalation occurs, you could talk together about which weapons you never want to use. Couples can agree on what their specific lines are—to never fight in front of their children, to never let an argument linger over two days, to never bring up the past in a current disagreement, to never make derogatory

comments about family members, and so forth—whatever both parties feel is a line that will work for them. The more protections you put in place by agreeing on boundaries that won't be crossed, the less likely your fights will escalate. It's important that both parties take responsibility to watch for line crossing, and that you have a plan of action to take if someone does cross one.

Let me stress something important, though: This negotiation must take place during a peaceful moment, *outside* the context of a fight. You can't have a real discussion when you're furious or when you can tell that your partner is about to reach for that historical bomb or WMD. So find a quiet time—perhaps in the aftermath of a fight, while you're both regretting how it went—when you both feel calm enough to talk about it. For obvious reasons, setting lines not to cross doesn't work if one partner attempts to set the rules for the other; lines must be mutual to work. In addition, it's important to also discuss how to recover if a line gets crossed in the heat of the battle. After a line has been crossed in one fight, it becomes easier to cross it again in the next one—unless you take steps to understand the desperation and pain that led to it and recommit to decommissioning that weapon.

INTERRUPTING AN ESCALATING FIGHT

Sometimes, escalated arguments happen despite your best efforts. So what about during the heat of the moment? How can you stop a fight *as* it's escalating? Stopping an Escalating Fight midstream is very, very difficult, especially when you consider what's happening in your head during such a fight. For most people it looks something like this:

When the animal-instinct part of your brain is firing in the midst of a fight, there's a lot of static and it becomes hard to think clearly or say things that make sense. You're unable to return to your more logical human self because all you feel is the pain. Your fight-or-flight system quickly turns your hurt into rage and prompts you to counterattack instantly. Slowing down this automatic reaction becomes the challenge. Sometimes, a part of you *is* aware of the damage that's occurring, even as you feel powerless to stop it. Figuring out how to recognize and listen to that part of you is key to slowing down an argument that's getting out of hand.

A desire for revenge and a need to win are two strong engines that drive people to escalate fights. It takes time and introspection (and sometimes working with a therapist) to understand the role that vengeance or winning-at-all-costs plays in your life. If you want to keep your fights from escalating, it's essential to learn to tolerate hurt without automatically retaliating and to allow yourself to back down and not have the last word.

Although it can seem nearly impossible to interrupt an Escalating Fight, here are some tools to try that can help:

TOOL 1: INITIATE A MUTUALLY AGREED TIME-OUT WITH AN "UNUSUAL FIGHT-STOPPING REMINDER"

A couple I worked with once joked, "When one of our fights gets going, I wish you could parachute in and referee it!" In the heat of the battle, we sometimes wish that someone with a cooler head could step in and call a time-out. Calling a time-out during a fight can be an excellent way to slow things down and stop the escalation. Unfortunately, a time-out called by just one of the combatants doesn't often work. One party might feel ready to end the argument and ask for it to stop, but if the other party is still fired-up in fight-or-flight mode, he or she might not be able to calm down quite yet.

Indeed, the time-out request is sometimes deployed as a way to have the last word—you say your last dig and then call a time-out. Or, it's called with genuinely good intentions, but your partner reads it as a tactic to shut off their next point, enflaming the fight. A time-out that *both* parties want is a time-out that works best—neither feels shut down and both feel the relief of a break from the escalation. But how can two people simultaneously call for a time-out?

During a calm, quiet moment, agree with your partner on a mutual "fire extinguisher" that you can bring into the room that represents your joint wish to keep from escalating. Choose an object or a word or phrase—preferably something a little random or weird that might inject some humor at a tough moment. The deal is, you agree that when one of you brings that object into the room or mentions the code word, that person is saying, "Please, please, let's remember that we want to pause a fight like this so that we can stop hurting each other. Let's take a break and revisit this when we are calmer." When the object is brought into the room or your specific phrase is uttered, both parties agree to stop talking, go to separate rooms, and cool off.

Bringing an object in is not a sure-fire way to stop an escalated fight, particularly if one party uses it with the intention of quieting the other. The reminder only works when it is a symbol of the *mutually* agreed upon effort to stop escalation.

TOOL 2: SAY "OUCH"

Each shot fired during an Escalating Fight originates from a bruised feeling: "You just hurt me with that insulting comment, so I'm going to fire something mean back at you." Rather than revealing that we were pained by what our partner said, we tend to *act* on that pain instead. The hurt goes in, and retaliation comes out.

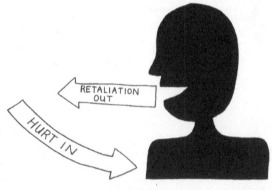

Sometimes this occurs because everything happens so quickly, but sometimes it's because we don't want to admit to feeling hurt. One of the partners in a couple I once counseled described this experience so well: "I can't show her how her comment hurt me—then she'd know she got a good one in." Revealing the pain she caused felt like weakness to him, so he would rather fire back and feel temporarily stronger again.

What would change if, when the hurt went in, an expression of that hurt came out?

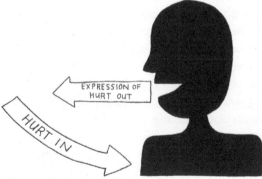

The couple here is in the middle of a particularly nasty Escalating Fight. Check out the difference in the outcome when one partner verbalizes her pain instead of striking back:

By slowing down your reactive tendencies enough to express the hurt before acting on it, you might have a shot at slowing down this kind of argument. Think about it: In a fast-paced Escalating Fight, the bombs are flying, but no one stops to hear the explosions. You quickly hurl harsh words and the receiver throws others right back. If it's not apparent that someone has been hurt, the impact doesn't register to the bomb-thrower. In a strange way, it's almost as if we need to see the result of the injuries we inflict to stop. Not seeing the pain in the other person can leave you with the sensation that you need to hurt your partner more. Over time, you become desensitized to how hurtful your words are and you can convince yourself that what you're saying means nothing. If it means nothing, you don't apologize, you don't feel remorse, and you eliminate any consciousness that might stop you the next time.

As the recipient of a bomb, you have a choice: Hide your reaction and retaliate, or show how shattered you feel. When your partner actually sees the impact he or she had on you, it can pause the fight and possibly stop it altogether. I encourage couples to practice communicating their hurt at the moment it happens. Choose to cry out, whimper, or say "ouch," rather than hit back. Or announce, "What you just said really hurts. I feel like striking back, but I don't want to keep this going, so I'm just going to tell you that I'm hurt." When both parties can do this, the argument slows down and a healing post-fight discussion becomes possible.

Preventing and pausing Escalating Fights are essential relationship skills, but they're not enough to deal with the sheer complexity of the full range of fights. In the next chapter, we'll look beyond the choice of weapons and begin to better understand the dynamics that drive fights.

THE ESCALATION FIGHT TOOLBOX

Prevent Escalation:

Agree on a plan that outlines "lines not to cross" and "weapons not to use" with specific examples.

Pause Escalation:

Choose an unusual fight-stopping reminder that will help you call for a mutual time-out.

Express the hurt you experience mid-fight instead of just retaliating.

CHAPTER 5

THE HOUSEHOLD RESPONSIBILITIES FIGHT

AT THE BEGINNING OF **A** relationship, partners are eager to do nice things for one another. They buy gifts, cook meals, and do little favors with pleasure. There's sweetness and love in helping your partner with the ordinary tasks in life.

When a couple decides to marry or live together, there's joy and plenty of generosity in setting up their shared home.

But then the years go by and the scene starts to look vastly different. . . .

What happened? How did all the cheerful cleaning, cooking, and running of errands turn into complaints and bickering? At some point, the tasks around the house were done with enthusiasm—joy, even—but later on, resentment, anger, and arguing take over. The Household Responsibility Fight almost always travels along this path.

A person living alone has to take care of all the responsibilities of a home on his or her own. Since there's no one with whom to divide the tasks, a single person figures out a way to get it all done (or not!). As soon as you have a roommate or a partner, though, it's natural to assume that the work will somehow be shared.

Of course, it doesn't always work out that way. Often without planning it, partners fall into routines, with each partner doing certain tasks more and others less. As life together goes on and gets more complicated, household tasks can pile up and the distribution of work can grow lopsided, especially if a couple hasn't previously discussed who is in charge of what. The drudgery of doing the same chores over and over becomes aggravating and, at some point, someone starts to feel that he or she is doing more than the other person, or too many of the most unpleasant tasks. And then the trouble starts.

Here's how the situation looks between Jeanette and Maxine:

Jeanette works remotely from home and has flexible work hours. Maxine commutes into the city daily, leaving early in the morning and returning late in the evening. Given their work schedules, it's always been easy for Jeanette to do little things around the house, like throw in a load of laundry when she gets up from her home office desk, or fold it while on a conference call. And it's been easier for Maxine to stop to get the groceries and dry cleaning on her way home from the city. It's made sense for Jeanette to get dinner started before Maxine gets home. And sure, Jeanette can let the plumber or other workers in when something needs to be fixed. Or pick up a prescription, and walk the dog. But over time, Jeanette has grown increasingly resentful that she's doing more than her fair share of the housework. Enter the Household Responsibilities Fight.

Like many couples, Jeanette and Maxine have veered into a distribution of household responsibilities that doesn't feel equally comfortable. Sometimes it happens because it works out that one partner is home more. Sometimes it happens because partners have different assumptions about what needs to get done or how it should get done, or because a couple has different views on what each partner is "supposed to do," according to cultural expectations. No matter the cause, once one partner starts to feel that the situation is unfair, he or she is likely to mention it, either explicitly or implicitly, by asking for help or complaining about it. Like most people who perceive unfairness, Jeanette vents because she wants Maxine to see her frustration, to agree that it's unfair, and to work with her to make things more equal.

Whatever happened to 50-50? You never do anything around here! I'm sick of taking care of everything for you!

Oh, I'm sorry! That really isn't fair to you! Let's sit down and figure out what I can take over.

This is the response Jeanette craves, and perhaps a more saintly partner out there might indeed respond in this wholly supportive way.

Unfortunately, reality often looks more like this:

Whatever happened to 50-50? You never do anything around here! I'm sick of taking care of everything for you!

Oh, don't be such a martyr! I do plenty of stuff too. And I never asked you to do all that stuff... you must just... LIKE to.

What causes Maxine to respond in this frustrated and angry way?

Part of it has to do with how Jeanette is starting the conversation. When Jeanette complains, Maxine feels accused by what she hears in the subtext of Jeanette's complaint.

Jeanette's initial intent is reasonable—she feels painfully overwhelmed and wants Maxine to help lighten her load, but her complaint has a bad impact on Maxine. As in Partner Improvement Fights (see Chapter 1), Jeanette's judgment comes through to Maxine. Understandably, what Maxine hears loudest is the insult, "You never do anything around here!" Jeanette appears to be *blaming* her for the uneven distribution of household responsibilities. This feels unfair because Maxine knows that in no way has she forced Jeanette to take on everything she does. In response, Maxine defends herself and throws an accusation back at Jeanette.

Oh, don't be such a **MARTYR**! I do plenty of stuff too. And I never asked you to do all that stuff...you must just...**LIKE** to.

Oh **REALLY?!?** So I'm here having a **PARTY** doing laundry and cleaning bathrooms ??

Here we go again ... always complaining. I never said I wouldn't help you out - just tell me what to do, boss, and I'll do it.

I don't want you to "help ME out"! You should see what needs to be done and do it without me having to ask you for "help"!

Jeanette, of course, has an angry reaction to Maxine's angry reaction! To Jeanette, it feels like Maxine is somehow saying that her complaint isn't justified, which makes Jeanette even more upset. All Jeanette wanted was to even out the workload and to receive the slightest bit of compassion, but she got none of that. Jeanette leaves the argument completely stuck—still burdened with too much responsibility and now frustrated as well at not feeling understood by her partner.

Stewing on the situation, Jeanette may feel the need to complain even more. But she also feels a little hopeless about raising the subject with Maxine in the future since it went so badly last time.

Maxine, for her part, feels blindsided by Jeanette's complaints. She knows she can't do as much as Jeanette to help around the house because of her schedule, but she works incredibly hard at the office; it's not like she's out at the beach! Plus, she does try to pitch in whenever she has time, but that never seems to count with Jeanette.

Jeanette and Maxine each try to solve the problems that pain them: Jeanette wants to change things to be more even, and Maxine wants to defend herself against Jeanette's unjust accusations. The fight becomes circular.

As we saw in the Nagging-Tuning Out Fight in Chapter 3, once a fight is circular, it's much harder to stop. To change the cycle, both Maxine and Jeanette need to recognize that they're both contributing to the fight with their reactions and judgments about one another, and they both have to work to alter the cycle.

What about the more simple solutions to the Household Responsibilities Fight? Couldn't they just sit down and renegotiate who does what so that the distribution of work is more fair? For some couples, opening a dialogue about who does what, sorting through all the tasks that need to be completed, and then dividing them up can indeed bring the argument to an end.

For many couples, though, that doesn't work because there's more going on beneath this fight than just who does what at home. Although Jeanette was hoping for a redistribution of the housework, Maxine doesn't want to talk about that when she doesn't feel appreciated for what she already does! Somewhat understandably, she reasons: Why give more when what I'm already doing doesn't matter anyway? And certainly, Jeannette feels the same way; she thinks: No one seems to appreciate how much I'm giving, so I don't want to give as much anymore.

To go beyond the obvious solution and get to the true root of the problem in a Household Responsibilities Fight (and in other fights as well, for that matter), it's important to understand a common undercurrent: It's all about expectations and appreciation.

OBLIGATIONS AND EXPECTATIONS

Household responsibilities and earning money are the unavoidable business components of a love relationship, and the two "staff members" in the partnership must somehow figure out how to get all of it done. Some couples talk with pride about how they "share everything 50-50" and never fight about work around the house. But 50-50 is a tough standard for most couples to maintain over the long run, especially as life circumstances shift. Work schedules and situations change, children are born, and pets are adopted. Dividing tasks becomes less consciously decided and more about habits that just evolve. It becomes someone's "job" to change the kitty litter and someone's "job" to buy groceries. Each partner grows used to the routine and, understandably, each starts to *expect* that the other partner will do his or her "job." Often, once something becomes routine, the relationship dynamic shifts.

Here's Ron, just after he moved in with his girlfriend, trying to be a gentleman.

The act of taking out the trash gets a loving reaction—or at least a positive one. His partner, Lucy, is surprised by his unexpected offer and appreciates the care for her that it represents. Ron's generosity is met with delight.

After a couple of months, though, Ron is still taking out the trash, but Lucy sometimes doesn't notice or say anything. Ron's generosity no longer causes delight. (To be fair, of course, Lucy has also been doing things around the house that Ron no longer notices, but for now, we're just watching Ron.)

More time passes, and now it seems that the trash job has Ron's name on it. At this point Lucy *expects* Ron to take out the trash. Understandably, Ron begins to feel a little less eager about the chore—same trash, less motivation.

Lucy may not have explicitly said that she expects Ron to take out the trash, and she may mention the trash with the most innocent intentions and in the most neutral tone. Yet somehow he *senses* that she expects him to do it, which is enough. The trash task has been altered from Trash-as-Generosity to Trash-as-Expectation, and that causes a few things to change.

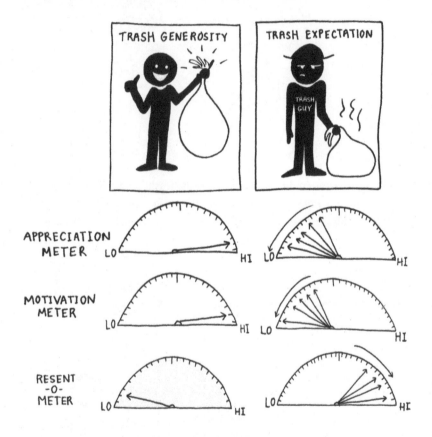

Once trash is Ron's "job" and Lucy *expects* him to do it, Lucy isn't likely to *express appreciation* for his effort. He's just doing his job, after all. It's become the routine, and thanking Ron for just following the routine seems like overkill, so like most people, she stops doing it. Perhaps she starts to believe that Ron doesn't mind doing the trash, so it's no great sacrifice on his part.

Without the extra ping of acknowledgment from Lucy, Ron's *energy* and *motivation* for taking the trash out will probably fade a bit—it's human nature. Doing a repetitive (and smelly) chore like the trash isn't self-rewarding enough for most people to stay excited about doing it. As a result, the potential for Ron to become *resentful* about taking out the trash grows.

THE PROBLEM WITH EXPECTATIONS

We all know it's not just about trash, though. This process can happen with any household responsibility—whether in the home or out. When you feel that what you're doing for your relationship has purpose and delights your partner, you want to keep doing it. This goes not only for doing chores, but for earning money in the partnership. When you feel that no one notices your contribution and takes it for granted, or expects you to do your "job" without complaining, it's harder to just keep doing it. The more partners speak about their roles in terms of expectations, the more generosity fades away.

It's ironic, really, because setting expectations is the most common thing people tend to do when they feel a partner isn't being generous enough! We say:

* ∗ "Here's what I need you to do. . . . "
* ∗ "If you would just. . . . "
* ∗ "I'm doing too much; I expect you to. . . . "

These expectation-laden requests make sense, of course, but they can have a paradoxical effect—they can *decrease* the likelihood that the partner who hears them will want to do what he or she is asked! This is how a Household Responsibilities Fight becomes more and more stuck over time. If you're *required* or simply *expected* to do the laundry, be the breadwinner, get up with the baby, or cook the food to someone else's standard, it all grows more onerous. Any of those activities could be things you used to do with a sense of pride in contributing to the relationship. But once you feel that sense of expectation or obligation from your partner, those tasks can become burdensome. Maxine may never have explicitly said that she expects Jeannette to do the laundry and many other household tasks, but over time as those tasks have become Jeannette's, it feels to Jeannette like she is *expected* to do them.

It's natural for someone who feels burdened to complain, ask for appreciation from the other, and solicit help. But those requests inevitably lead to more of the same problem, since trying to get your partner to be more generous by asking him or her to be so, by laying out or hinting at specific expectations, doesn't actually motivate him or her to be more generous. In fact, it hampers generosity.

Not surprisingly, then, household responsibilities become a battleground of obligations, expectations, and resentment. Everyone feels like they're doing too much and not getting enough back. At that point, the generosity, the offers to do more, and the expressions of appreciation begin to dry up. After enough revolutions around the cycle of expectation and disappointment, it can feel like you both exist in a land of chronic bad weather—a Climate of Resentment.

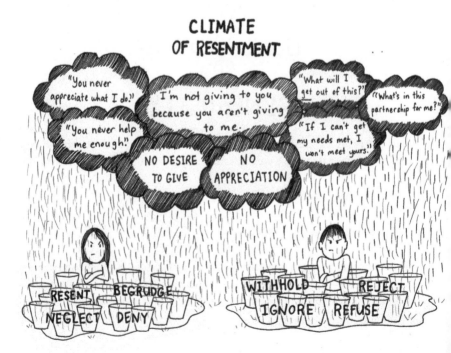

A Climate of Resentment feels terrible to both partners—neither one feels like the other is offering enough and each starts to focus more on what they're trying to *get* from the relationship rather than what they're willing to *give*. Neither partner wants to appreciate what the other does and it becomes every person for him or herself. Each acknowledges only what he or she contributes and sees nothing but selfishness on the other side.

What we all want instead, of course, is a chance to return back to the Climate of Generosity.

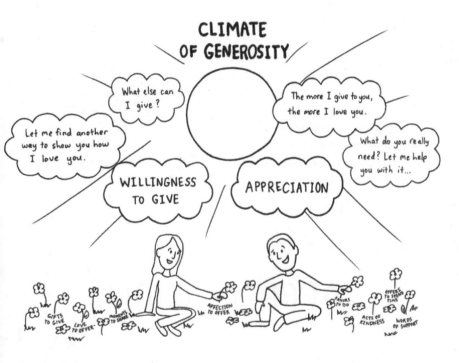

In a Climate of Generosity, there's a lot of giving and a lot of appreciation. It's all about showing your love and care, offering to your partner before you receive for yourself. It's the climate many couples remember fondly from the beginning of their relationship. As you fell in love, you would do anything for your partner. It was easy to freely express your appreciation, too.

So how can you get back to that? How do you change a Climate of Resentment into a Climate of Generosity? How do you reverse the tide to make both of you generous again? We all know that you can't change the weather outside. But "bad weather" in a relationship is cocreated, and it can be reversed.

First, it takes recognition.

To go from a Climate of Resentment to one of Generosity, both partners have to see that they're stuck. Often someone will say, "I'm still being generous. It's my partner who's being selfish!" Here's the catch, though: If you think your partner is being selfish, it implies that *you* have *expectations* that he or she isn't meeting. You expect your partner to do a particular kindness, but he or she doesn't, and it's easy to label that as selfishness. However, that way of thinking might mean that you're more deeply under the gray clouds than you think.

True generosity is about giving without resentment or expectation. If what you're "giving" isn't wholehearted anymore, there's probably a little expectation lurking somewhere in the undercurrent. The key to recreating a Climate of Generosity is to notice the ways you each exert expectations on your relationship and to make a joint commitment to stop. This is easier said than done: Expectations can be very hard to drop. It's human nature to want to ask for something from your partner if you feel it's missing. Once you see how expectations can work against you, how they can actually *prevent* you from getting what you want, it becomes a bit easier. In addition, you can infuse the climate with sunshine—that is, appreciation—from both sides. It's clichéd advice: Focus on appreciating all that your partner does, rather than resenting the things that are missing, but appreciation is the key to changing the climate.

The more appreciation that both partners infuse into the relationship, the more generosity each will feel like offering. But there's one more key ingredient to changing the climate, one we don't often think about: increasing the opportunities in the relationship to delight your partner.

THE OPPORTUNITY TO DELIGHT

Let's take a look at a couple early in their relationship, Andre and Sophia. When Andre brings home flowers for Sophia, he wants to surprise her and see the happy look on her face—and Sophia is delighted!

She loves the beautiful flowers, but even more so, she feels loved by Andre and happy that her guy thought of surprising her with flowers. Her excited reaction thrills Andre, too. He feels the wonderful joy of giving, and Sophia's delight means that his effort at communicating love was received and appreciated.

After this happy moment, Sophia might feel so loving toward Andre that she starts to consider what nice things she might do for Andre to please him. Perhaps Sophia decides to make his favorite food that night. The delicious dinner she cooks delights Andre, and not surprisingly he then feels motivated to delight her back. Off they go into the sunset, creating a happy cycle of love, doing sweet things for the other person, appreciating one another and feeling loved.

Everything is great for Sophia and Andre—unless *expectation* worms its way into the cycle:

This flower giving feels very different than before. Andre knows that Sophia is counting on getting flowers, and that knowledge sits somewhere in his mind as an expectation. When he buys flowers for her now, he doesn't feel the same anticipation of surprising her. Sophia might be quite happy with the flowers and also feel reassured that Andre loves her because he did what she asked. But it isn't quite as good as the feeling she'd have if she didn't have to tell him to get the flowers.

For Andre, the whole exchange feels considerably worse than when there was no expectation. Whatever delight he might cause by bringing flowers home is a bit tainted with the feeling that Sophia orchestrated his actions. He might be asking himself, "Is the delight I see in her face actually reflecting her satisfaction that she can control me?" No wonder he feels less generous next time!

Of course, when she asks for flowers, Sophia isn't trying to control Andre at all; she just hopes that by telling him she likes flowers he might buy them more often—which would make her feel happy more often. What she doesn't realize, though, is that when she tells him her wish, she is inadvertently adding expectation to the mix and draining the opportunity for Andre to delight her more authentically. The more she *expects* the romantic flowers, the less romantic they become.

As Andre gives Sophia the flowers that she expects, he might think: "You told me to get them for you, so if I get them for you, I meet your expectations; if I don't get them, I fail to meet your expectations. There's no scenario where I get to *exceed* your expectations." It's either failure or just barely passing.

Once a couple has been through many cycles of expectation and disappointment, the partners begin to assume disappointment will happen. The neutral question, "Hi, how was your day?" has no apparent expectation in it. But, below, this husband assumes his wife is *thinking* about her expectations and it is enough for him feel its negative effects. The opportunity to delight shrinks. The higher the expectation, the greater the opportunity to fail and the less room to exceed expectations or to delight your partner.

When considering household responsibilities, it might seem like a stretch to say that loading the dishwasher will "delight" your partner—but knowing that your partner appreciates your effort does make doing it more worthwhile. Feeling appreciated as the breadwinner for your family can keep you plugging away at a job you hate; after all, it still feels good to be providing. Knowing that your partner will enjoy good food and a clean home can also carry you through the unpleasant moments of going grocery shopping in the rain or cleaning toilets. The key, then, to maintaining a Climate of Generosity around household responsibilities is to find lots of ways to preserve the opportunity to delight by keeping expectations to a minimum and showing appreciation for one another's contributions.

For Maxine and Jeanette, the first step was to acknowledge that they were stuck in a Household Responsibility Fight under a dark cloud of resentment.

To tip the climate back to one of generosity, Jeanette carefully considers how she can start a conversation with Maxine about rebalancing the household tasks.

By consciously setting her mindset to create a positive climate by *being generous*, Jeanette has the best chance of encouraging Maxine to respond with generosity. Here's how it played out:

I've got to drop resentment and expectations and give and appreciate more.

Maxine, I'm feeling overwhelmed with all the housework. I know we didn't plan it this way but I'm ending up doing a lot and it's getting hard.

Leaves opportunity for Maxine to make a suggestion of how to solve the problem, no expectations, just a request to discuss

I didn't realize it bothered you. You have been doing a lot and I appreciate it. It's been so nice that you've made all those dinners.

Generous with appreciation and acknowledging the contribution

I actually love making dinner and I'm happy to keep doing that. I know you love it too. But some of the other stuff is making me feel resentful and I don't want to be.

Generosity, preserving delight, and working to avoid resentment

Got it. What can I do that would help you feel better quickest?

I've got to give and appreciate more and drop expectations and resentment

Thank you! I feel better already. What would you feel best about doing?

Generous with appreciation and no expected solution

Giving with attention to taking care of Jeanette's pain as the priority

I actually don't mind laundry that much - would that help?

GENEROSITY

That would be awesome!

DELIGHT!

Jeanette begins by describing her frustration *without* accusing Maxine. She even acknowledges that Maxine is *not* the cause of the unequal distribution of work. (Notice the difference between the start of this conversation and the "What happened to 50-50?" version earlier in this chapter.) Maxine, who also wants to create a climate of generosity, answers with appreciation and shows a willingness to discuss it further.

Throughout the conversation, Jeanette and Maxine both focus on finding ways to appreciate and to give. There are moments in this dialogue where either one of them could get annoyed at what their partner is saying, so they also display generosity by letting those comments roll off their backs.

To change the climate, both sides have to change. As the partner who currently does less housework, Maxine could find ways to give more in that realm, to offer more spontaneous appreciation for all Jeanette does, and to see Jeanette's contributions more as gifts ("laundry-as-generosity") than as business-as-usual ("laundry-as-expectation"). Jeanette's contribution to a Climate of Generosity could be to offer what she's already doing with a positive attitude of giving rather than resentment, and to step away from a mindset full of expectations that erases any possibility for delight. In addition, Jeanette could more actively acknowledge how Maxine is already contributing around the house and with her income. Both partners would remember what makes doing chores more tolerable: knowing that your work has a purpose and is appreciated and not just expected.

Household responsibilities, including the monetary part of those responsibilities, are particularly susceptible to being taken for granted. It takes conscious attention to keep those tasks infused with appreciation and the opportunity to delight. The tasks themselves may not hold any charm, but if doing them makes someone you love happy, they become worth doing. Appreciation and delight elevate responsibilities into love.

THE HOUSEHOLD RESPONSIBILITIES FIGHT TOOLBOX

 How you raise problems about household fairness makes a big difference in how feedback is received.

 A Climate of Resentment is fueled by efforts to get the other person to be more generous through criticism and expectations.

 A Climate of Generosity is fueled by appreciating your partner and being generous in your words and actions.

EXPECTATION KILLS GENEROSITY

APPRECIATION INSPIRES GENEROSITY INSPIRES

CHAPTER 6

THE BIRTHDAY FIGHT

SARA LOVES HER BIRTHDAY. It's always carried special significance to her—she happily recollects memories of family celebrations and of friends going out of their way to be thoughtful and create surprises. "So why did I end up with the one guy who doesn't have a clue how to celebrate a birthday?" she asks herself. In the early years of their relationship, when Ed would get her a dumb card or an odd present (A salad spinner?! Really??), she laughed it off as quirky or adorably clueless, but now it seems like he just doesn't care enough to actually put thought into it.

It's my birthday. He should do something special, but he'll probably mess it up again. I should help him... but I still wish he would think of it on his own.

Since it's important to her, she tries to explain to him why birthdays matter. She has asked with sincerity if he could please put more effort into it next year. Amazingly, he managed to forget what she'd said, and this year did no better. He thought that the nice dinner they had the week before her birthday "counted" as the celebration.

Over the years, Sara has become increasingly frustrated as she builds up some hope for her birthday and then finds herself disappointed yet again. For Sara, this is bigger than just her birthday—it feels like another example of how Ed doesn't show any appreciation or affection for her. Sometimes, she tries to help him: hinting sweetly about things she might like or reminding him in advance that her birthday is approaching, but that doesn't seem to go very far. One year, she gave him a foolproof way to get it right. A week before her birthday, she offered him a specific idea about what he could get her and how they could celebrate. So he planned the dinner at the restaurant she wanted and got the gift she requested, but then he kept asking over and over if Sara liked what he did. "He was like a little kid asking for approval. It was all about him."

Ed thinks that Sara has "an issue" about her birthday. She always wants a big hoopla, which seems childish to him. But he knows that if he doesn't play the game and buy the card, the cake, and the decorations, if he doesn't plan the perfect outing and buy the perfect gift, she'll give him hell for it—and he would rather avoid that. Even when he tries to do the birthday things he knows she wants, somehow it never meets her standards; it's never right, or never enough. Some years, the tension starts a full month before her birthday.

He can sense that she's building up her expectations, and he just knows that somehow he'll fail again and there will be a fight. He tries to make her birthday a priority, but admittedly, he sometimes forgets and rushes to make up for it at the last minute. Once, exasperated, he tried to explain that it's a little unreasonable to expect the world to stop completely on Sara's Big Day in May in order to follow her instructions, but that didn't go over well—she cried and avoided him for days. One year, he thought he'd go the extra mile by making her a cake instead of buying it, but work got busy and he didn't gather the ingredients until the morning of her birthday. When he started making the cake that morning, she was annoyed that he was messing up the kitchen. "Even if I put in a ton of effort, there's just no way to win," he thinks.

Both Sara and Ed are frustrated that the other person keeps doing the same annoying thing year after year.

STUCK IN A BAD CYCLE

Sara and Ed have legitimately different ideas about how birthdays should be celebrated, and that difference is one of the root causes of this fight. But after a few birthdays where things don't go well, the fight becomes frustratingly locked up as circular dynamics take over.

To examine the problem more closely, let's start with Sara. She's thinking about her upcoming birthday and carries with her the cloud of her previous birthday disappointments.

She can't help it; driven by her not-unreasonable desire to have a great birthday celebration, she tries various actions at different times leading up to the day—sometimes hinting, sometimes directing, sometimes testing, and sometimes complaining. It's not surprising that a person might want their partner to make a fuss over a birthday, and Sara is right that Ed hasn't done a great job in the past. Unintentionally, though, the actions Sara takes to get what she wants puts a lot of pressure on Ed, which drives him away from wanting to make that fuss. Her actions also inadvertently reinforce Ed's view that Sara is unreasonably controlling about her birthday.

Let's look at the situation from Ed's perspective. He's right, too. The past fights he and Sara have had about birthdays have steadily built up the pressure on him to an excruciating level.

He's come to think of Sara's birthday requests as either subtly manipulative, or outright controlling. Carrying around the weight of the pressure, Ed tries to figure out a way to feel less burdened by it. Sometimes, that means putting it totally out of his mind, or putting off dealing with it, or even letting Sara know she can't control him. Other times he just gives in and does exactly what she says because he can't stand the complaining anymore. It's understandable that Ed, who feels controlled, finds ways to avoid giving in to the pressure, perhaps by not immediately doing what's asked of him or by trying to tell Sara that her request is too much. Unintentionally, though, the actions Ed takes to feel less pressure create disappointment for Sara, making her feel unimportant and fueling her view that Ed is hopeless at caring or giving.

Neither Ed nor Sara intends to create this awful cycle, but their methods of attempting to fix the problem repeatedly backfire. They each contribute to the fight cycle, whether intentionally or not. Recognizing this is the first critical step to stopping the fight. Once they are aware that they each play a role in the perpetuation of this cycle, they can *both* take steps to stop it.

But just stopping what they're *doing* isn't enough. As in the Nagging-Tuning Out Fight (see Chapter 3), both partners have to change their *thinking*, to have a less judgmental mindset about one another. To do this, they need some additional insight into the other person's feelings and how the dynamics of circular fights begin.

HOW BAD CYCLES START

Both Ed and Sara are good people at heart. They have good intentions and good values. Sure, they have some flaws and fears, and can be sensitive to certain things, but at the core, they're good.

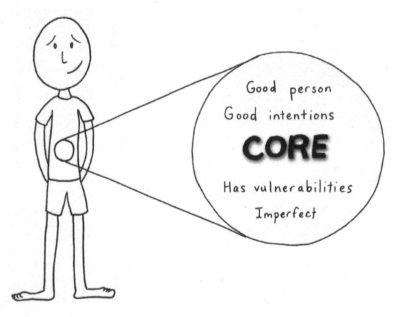

At the core, they both generally operate with positive intentions as they try to realize their hopes and dreams. They're imperfect and sometimes make mistakes, but they both want to love and be loved and to be a good partner to the other.

In the beginning of the relationship, Ed and Sara's actions seemed to come directly from the heart of who they are. Back then, their good intentions showed through in kind and passionate ways. They were easily generous and loving to one another, with the true desire to delight their partner. They could even show the imperfect parts of their selves to one another, taking risks to share real feelings and maybe even some of their fears or vulnerabilities. When they were falling in love, they could reveal a secret or a weakness and they'd receive acceptance and love from the other person. Sharing from their cores bonded them together, and it felt great.

During this time, Ed and Sara were acting in what we'll call Core Mode—a mode of action where your actions are driven by the real you, without anxiety or fear.

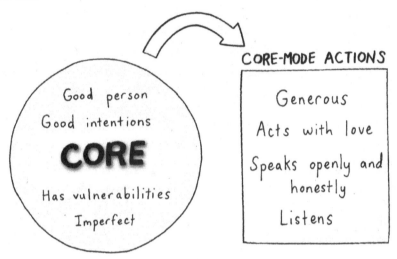

CORE-MODE ACTIONS

Good person
Good intentions
CORE
Has vulnerabilities
Imperfect

Generous
Acts with love
Speaks openly and honestly
Listens

When both partners are in Core Mode, they can easily listen to one another and tolerate the other person's mistakes or quirks, recognizing that they come from a well-intended place. ("She was late meeting me at the party, but I know it's just because she had important things to do at work. She's so ambitious and I think that's great!")

In Core Mode, Ed and Sara even saw one another's quirks positively: "Sara is so cute about celebrations—she loves all those romantic touches, which I just love!" or "Ed is so genuine and laid back, and he doesn't sweat the small stuff— I love that about him." If Ed and Sara were able to stay in Core Mode all the time, they would have fewer fights. But another mode of behavior that we all frequently fall into causes some real trouble: Defense Mode.

We're built, biologically, to be able to survive in the face of threats. When something threatens our physical survival, we strike back, run away, or find some other way to protect ourselves. Threats like tigers, lightning storms, or other humans with spears will trigger our fight-or-flight systems, but so do threats of a more social or emotional nature. When our feelings are hurt or warm connections to others are interfered with by the act of another person,

we sense that as a threat, too. Those threats pop us out of Core Mode as we try
to find a way to protect ourselves. In other words, we enter Defense Mode.

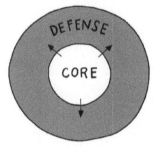

For example, if another person criticizes you or tries to control you, you experience a visceral threat. When you feel left out, misunderstood, abandoned, or disrespected, your brain activates the same fight-or-flight system it would if an
earthquake erupted beneath you. No one is immune from feeling these threats,
though for each person certain threats land more painfully than others.

Threats come at you like pointy, sharp attacks on your core; they're painful and they feel dangerous. Naturally, we jump to protect and defend ourselves against them. We all hurt when we're ignored, insulted, or injured and, understandably, we look for a way to strike back or gain space to lessen the pain.

Each type of threat has its own typical, predictable response. If you criticize me, I might criticize you back. If you embarrass me, I might avoid you in the future. If I think you'll abandon me, I might cling more tightly. If you crowd me, I might want to make extra space for myself. If you make me feel irrelevant, I might exert my importance.

These reflexes are quite logical, and anyone who feels like they're under attack from these particular threats is likely to have a similar reaction. Consequently, defensive actions feel very justified given the threat. "I had to say something back—he totally insulted me!" Justified. "She was ignoring me—I had to get her to pay attention again!" Justified.

In the Birthday Fight, Sara sees Ed's lackluster approach to her big day as a sign that he's stopped caring about her as much as he used to, which is scary for her.

She fears, "If he can't show his love on my birthday, maybe his love for me is fading. . . ." That worry threatens her, and she can't bear it. So she tries to help Ed be better at celebrating her birthday. That way, he can demonstrate that his love is alive and well, and she'll feel more confident that she's in a loving, stable relationship.

Sara's Defense Mode Actions—hinting, reminding, and even prescribing what Ed should do for her—are all a response to the threat she perceives. Her behavior is understandable and reasonable; when faced with a feeling of a diminishing connection, it's human nature to try to rebuild it.

The problem is that Sara's actions then create a threat for Ed. Every time she suggests or dictates instructions for her birthday, Ed feels judged and controlled: "She's telling me that I no longer make her happy and that nothing I do for her is good enough. And then she tries to use me like a puppet just to do what she wants!"

Ed hates feeling like a failure in Sara's eyes, so he does what people often do in the face of likely or certain failure—he stops trying. Perhaps he avoids thinking about it until the last minute or he makes nothing more than a halfhearted attempt; after all, "why put effort into it if she'll never be happy anyway?" Also, by *not* doing what Sara wants, he can shake off that feeling that she's in command of his actions.

Both Ed and Sara are trying to solve the problem they perceive. Ed feels less like a failure when he doesn't try so hard, and Sara feels less risk of losing Ed's devotion if she "helps him" with all her hints and reminders. The problem is, of course, that their Defense Mode Actions create new threats for the other person—there's more of the judgment and hints of control that hurt Ed, and more fear for Sara that Ed has stopped caring about her. Taking defensive actions when you feel threatened is rather automatic, and it's focused on stopping your *own* pain. It would take effort for Sara and Ed to recognize their defensive actions against their partner. It's not easy to see the whole cycle when you are in it. As we saw in the Proving Your Point Fight in Chapter 2, the *intent* behind being defensive is understandable, but the *impact* of your defensive actions creates trouble.

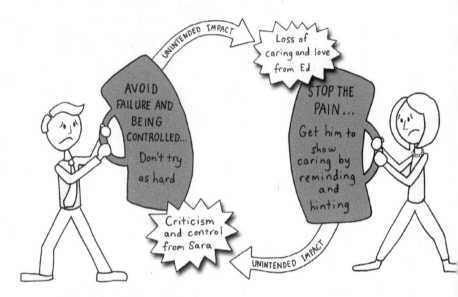

If Ed's Defense Mode Actions create a threat to Sara, and Sara's Defense Mode Actions trigger a threat back to Ed, it's easy to see how the Birthday Fight becomes worse over time. The perceived threats begin to feel bigger and bigger as the defensive measures grow more extreme. The fight is not only circular—it also *escalates* over time.

your Defense is my THREAT

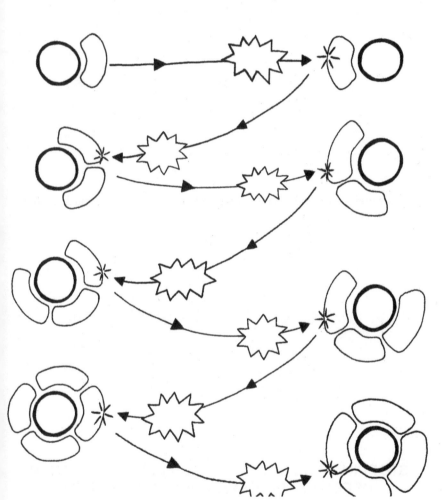

When I explain the concepts of Core Mode and Defense Mode to the couples I work with, they see it right away: "Yes, that's exactly what happens! I feel hurt, and I know I get defensive. My partner does, too. We just can't stop it."

Together, they recognize the issue—they're stuck in Defense Mode, endlessly triggering one another, caught in a vicious cycle.

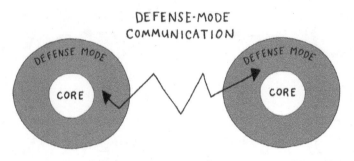

They understand, too, that the fix is to figure out how to go back to communicating Core-to-Core.

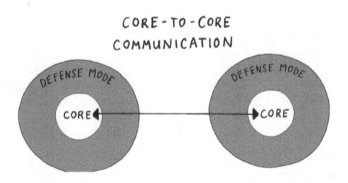

STOPPING THE BIRTHDAY FIGHT (OR ANY OTHER DEFENSE-TRIGGERED CIRCULAR FIGHT)

The return to Core-to-Core Communication begins with a Repairing Conversation. Most of us know that when interpersonal interactions start to feel uncomfortable, whether at work or at home, the right thing to do is to "sit down and talk about it." Beyond the "sitting down" part, though, it can be difficult to know what to do next. The "talking" part is all about finding your way back to Core-to-Core Communication, and here's how you can do that:

THE REPAIRING CONVERSATION

Step 1: Recognize the Mutual Defense Mode

Once you start to think about Defense Mode, it's not hard to recognize when you're stuck in it. You know it when conversations revolve around the same old argument, or when you say things you know you'll regret later. *Anything* you say seems to trigger the other person, and anger and hurt continue to build rather than subside. That's Defense Mode, and you can't break free from it unless you notice you're in it. Calling attention to Defense Mode can't be one-sided, though. If you try to stop the fight by telling your partner to "stop being so defensive," you'll very likely make things worse. It's *mutual* Defense Mode that is actually the cause of the never-ending fights. The fix, then, is for both parties to take responsibility for their contributions to Defense Mode and to make a joint commitment to return to Core-to-Core Communication.

To break out of a Defense Mode cycle, it is critical for both partners to get a full understanding of the Big Picture of what is happening and to understand all parts of the cycle from both sides: the threats you each are responding to, the Defense Mode Actions you each are taking that trigger the other, and what you are both feeling at the core. Once you understand all of the pieces, you can focus on supporting each other's core feelings, which makes the need to be defensive slowly lessen.

Step 2: Recognize the Threats Your Defense Mode Actions Cause

Unintentionally or not, you've both hurt one another as you tried to protect yourself. When you can each acknowledge that you understand how your actions may have landed painfully on your partner, it's a great relief, and the warm connection begins to rebuild.

> I guess my prodding and reminding could feel ∿controlling∿ to you—- I get that it might get irritating. Is that what you feel?

> I know you feel hurt when it seems I don't get my act together about your birthday. I get that it makes you feel I ∿don't care∿ Is that it?

Both partners recognize the unfortunate impact they had on each other. Ed doesn't intend to let Sara down on her birthday or imply that he doesn't care about her; he's just responding to the threats *he* feels. But he still understands that his behavior had a bad impact on Sara. Sara doesn't intend to threaten Ed with criticism; she's responding to the threats *she* feels. Still, she sees now that her criticism hurt Ed.

Step 3: Commit to Stopping Defensive Actions

Once you recognize the specific Defense Mode Actions you each engage in that drive the negative cycle, you can commit to work on stopping those actions. It isn't easy, of course, since defensive actions can get fairly automatic. However, deciding together to put down the defensive shields when an issue comes up is an initial step toward beginning to trust one another again. When both sides step out of their Defense Modes, there are fewer threats to defend against and the cycle begins to unravel.

Sara and Ed eventually recognized how each of their actions in the Birthday Fight had an unintended bad impact on the other person and made a commitment to stop doing them. For Sara, this meant no more hinting and reminding Ed about her birthday, no more requests that sounded like controlling instructions, and no more comments that implied that Ed was a hopeless failure or didn't really care. For Ed, changing his defensive behavior meant no longer complaining about Sara's opinion on birthdays, making sure to take action rather than avoiding birthday planning, and putting more of his true feelings about Sara into his birthday plans for her. When both Sara and Ed stopped their unproductive and often harmful actions, they took a monumental step toward de-escalating their fight. But it isn't enough to bring them back to their cores.

Step 4: Understand What Is Core for You

Ed and Sara each need to do a bit of excavation inside themselves to understand what truly underlies their fight. What is going on in their cores that made them feel so threatened in this fight?

As we saw earlier, for Sara this fight isn't just about her birthday. How her birthday is celebrated feels like a symbol of how much Ed cares for her. How much time and energy is he willing to spend in order to delight her? How frequently does she occupy his thoughts? How special is she to him, really? Every little thing that Ed does for her birthday is like an extra piece of evidence to prove that he truly loves her.

THE REAL SARA

I want to feel special and know you love me. I want to be able to receive without feeling guilty.

There's more, too. In her core, Sara craves the feeling of being special to Ed, but she's also afraid of being too demanding. She often feels that she gives more than she gets in life, and her birthday is the one day when she feels justified in expecting a lot from others, without feeling guilty—it is her *birthday*, after all. The Birthday Fight is especially hard for her because she always feels torn between longing to feel special and trying to avoid feeling guilty for asking for too much.

When Sara feels abandoned or not cared about, that hurt causes her to try to avoid disappointment by taking matters into her own hands, which takes the form of directing Ed to do all the things that make her feel loved and cared for. When she feels let down, she might also complain as a way to try to influence Ed. Then, when she feels she's being too demanding, she abruptly withdraws all effort and waits to see what happens. But, if Sara can understand the reasons behind her personal feelings about birthdays, especially in the context of her relationship with Ed, she can help Ed understand them, too.

Ed does some serious thinking as well. He knows he truly loves Sara, but he hates being pressured into doing something that doesn't mean much to him; it feels artificial. He'd rather show his love when the mood strikes him, when he feels it most strongly—not on a required schedule. Sure, he'd like to make Sara's birthday special for her, but even when he tries, he's genuinely amazed that something always manages to get in the way of him following through on his plans. It's as if his brain just turns off when it comes to Sara's birthday. After digging below the surface a bit, he thinks, "Maybe my brain turns off because I know I'll never get it right, so it wonders why I should even try."

THE REAL ED

I wish I could be good at this stuff but I fear I'm not. I don't like feeling like I don't please you and I don't want to be a failure.

In his core, Ed loves Sara and wants to be giving, but he's also sensitive to feeling like a failure, and the Birthday Fight leaves him feeling like he'll never get it right. When faced with the feeling of failure previously in his life, Ed has learned to defend against it by allowing himself to not care about whatever he's failing at. When Sara complains about the restaurant he chose for her birthday, it hits him where it hurts—she's saying out loud that he failed. That punch to his pride causes him to defend himself by striking back, telling Sara that she's being unreasonable, selfish, and demanding.

An important note about understanding your core and the threats you feel: It's not always easy to identify the specific threats that cause your defensive actions or the deeper feelings that underlie the threats. Sometimes it helps to have a therapist work with you to figure out what you're responding to so that you can describe it to your partner. An important first goal of couple's therapy is often to uncover the Defense Mode cycle and have both parties understand, on a deep level, the threats that drive it.

Step 5: Speak from Your Core—Tell Your Partner What You Feel

When you and your partner first discuss resolving the fight, start with what you feel in your core, the real heart of it—what you long for, what makes you feel vulnerable, and what worries you. Speaking from your core does *not* mean describing your deep annoyance at your partner's defensive behavior (saying, for example, "I'm deeply hurt that you never celebrate my birthday" just perpetuates the threat). Speaking from your core is about expressing your deep wish or concern *directly*.

Step 6: Understand What Is Core for Your Partner

Stopping the fight requires an important mindset shift. Typically, when we have been fighting about an issue for a long time, all we see is this:

It's a key mindset change to see threats that come your way like this:

Instead of just being annoyed about a threat coming from your partner, you begin to wonder: What is it about my partner's core that causes him to defend himself this way (which then triggers me)? Recognizing that your partner's actions (e.g., procrastination, avoidance, complaining, or nagging) are coming from their defensive layer, rather than their core, opens the possibility that they could find a way back to a better, core way of being! If Sara stepped back to reflect, she'd find herself wondering:

> There must be a good reason why an otherwise reliable guy like Ed forgets to plan for my birthday. Maybe there's something ~threatening~ in it for him...

If Ed gave it another look, he'd become curious and think:

> There must be a good reason why an otherwise reasonable person like Sara gets so picky about her birthday. I wonder what feels ~threatening~ when she doesn't have the birthday she wants?

Figuring out what is core for your partner requires you to be curious about what lays *behind* what you actually see, and to ask questions that seek understanding. Admitting to your partner, "I don't think I fully understand what you're feeling; can you help me get what's happening for you?" or simply acknowledging that "there seems to be more to this story that I don't fully understand yet," helps open the door to locate what's in the other's core.

Understanding one another's core wishes, vulnerabilities, and defensive habits at this deeper level gives Ed and Sara the right mindset to stop the Birthday Fight.

Step 7: Act with Awareness

Here's where you show that you truly understand your partner's core. Now that you're aware of the threats that your partner is vulnerable to, your actions can reflect that knowledge. You can either talk about what you understand and find reasonable in your partner's core, or you can adapt your own actions based on what you know really matters to him or her. Acting with awareness of your partner's core means you're empathetic to his or her concerns and are willing to address those concerns or vulnerabilities.

Now when a birthday discussion comes up, Sara and Ed set their frame of mind first—reminding themselves of what is core to the other person and to themselves. Their actions will then spring from these generous mindsets, and the results are considerably better than ever before.

Sara keeps her focus on her core feeling—the desire to feel special with no guilty strings attached—and explains that to Ed. Ed hears her and knows that the pressure he felt before was just a result of her defensive actions, which arose out of her wish for a special birthday. He no longer interprets them as being about his shortcomings. Ed explains, with sincerity, that he loves Sara, and wants to please her without feeling the threat of failure. Sara hears him and works hard not to interpret his imperfect birthday celebration as uncaring.

On her next birthday, Ed uses his understanding of what Sara craves to guide how he plans for it.

What Ed actually ends up doing to celebrate Sara's birthday still may not be exactly what she was hoping for (a gift of a universal remote), but it's offered with a mindset of wanting to make her feel special on her birthday and the rest of the year.

Sara catches herself judging the gift and instead stops to recognize the mindset with which it's offered. When she lets Ed give to her in the way that feels right to him, she experiences less guilt about receiving, and that's a relief. She puts in extra effort to acknowledge what Ed does on his own initiative—not just on her birthday but all the time. And in the future, each time the frustrating cycle *doesn't* happen, they make sure they appreciate one another's changes, leaving both with a greater feeling that the fight won't happen again.

DEFENSE / CORE TOOLS FOR OTHER CYCLICAL FIGHTS

Using the example here of the Birthday Fight, you can see that these important tools can be employed to stop a wide variety of fights. Many recurring fights between couples are that way because both partners are stuck in Defense Mode and can't find their way back to understanding one another's core, let alone communicate Core-to-Core.

In fact, when couples describe the problems they have as "we just can't communicate with one another," it's often a clue that they're stuck in mutual Defense Modes. To stop these fights, consider that the annoying behaviors your partner shows can be signs of deep, important feelings (their core), which are showing up as irritating defensive actions. Once you listen at a deeper level and understand those feelings, the keys to ending the fight can emerge. So call a time-out, recognize that a bad cycle is happening, and work together to turn it around. Get curious about your own core, your partner's core, and the threats you each unwittingly pose that push the other person into Defense Mode. Both of you can then ask yourselves some difficult questions:

- What are the actions I take when I'm being defensive?

- How do my actions create threat for my partner?

- What could my partner's hurt feelings be about?

- What do I feel most hurt about?

- How do all these actions and feelings interact in a bad cycle?

Once you each have answers to these questions, sit down and discuss them together.

One final note: Understanding one another's core feelings sometimes requires deep effort; it's not a quick tool. Some couples might need to work with a therapist to get in touch with what's actually happening to each partner at their core. The effort is worth it, since Core-to-Core conversations lead to closer emotional bonds.

THE BIRTHDAY FIGHT TOOLBOX

 Recognize the fight cycle.

 Ask yourself the difficult questions.

 Commit to stopping defensive actions.

 Recognize the threats that trigger you and your partner's Defense Modes.

 Have a Repairing Conversation that connects from Core-to-Core.

CHAPTER 7

THE
BAD REPUTATION
FIGHT

NE EVENING, BRANDON WAS SICK with the flu. He wished that Arthur would skip his weekly poker game and maybe get him some soup. No such luck: Arthur, coming off of a rough day at work, went directly to his poker game. Left alone, Brandon felt hurt and angry.

When Arthur got home, Brandon complained, "How could you go out when you knew how sick I was? How could you care so little?"

Arthur thought this was unfair: "That's ridiculous! You're making way too big a deal about being a little sick."

"A little sick? I can barely breathe! But why would you care? You're a selfish jerk!"

"Oh, not this again." Arthur slammed the door as he left the room.

Brandon picked up the phone and called a mutual friend, Jared, to vent about Arthur's insensitivity. He knew that it might anger Arthur that he told someone else about the situation, but Brandon didn't care.

With each partner perceiving multiple threats from the other, Brandon and Arthur both go into Defense Mode and the fight escalates.

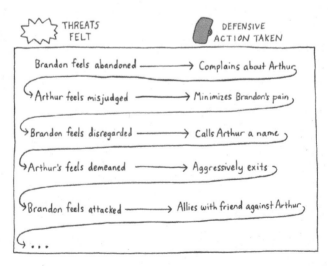

WHEN DEFENSIVE ACTIONS BUILD UP

This isn't the first time Brandon and Arthur have had a fight like this. They've had it many, many times before, and over time their defenses have built up. The more rounds they go, the more their defensive actions become a predictable mode of behavior, and the harder it becomes to step out of it.

DEFENSIVE ACTIONS BECOME HABITS

Because they've been through this argument so many times, Brandon and Arthur no longer flip between Core Mode and Defense Mode (see the Birthday Fight, Chapter 6). They start to stay in Defense Mode all the time, even when there's no specific threat at hand.

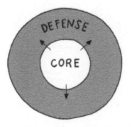

Arthur may start going straight from work to poker on a regular basis without calling home so that he can avoid receiving what he anticipates will be a guilt trip from Brandon. Brandon may complain about what Arthur will "probably" do when Brandon is sick before Arthur even has a chance to decide what he wants to do. Defense Mode becomes a habit in their relationship; it's their only way of interacting.

HABITS BECOME REPUTATIONS

Brandon already knows that Arthur will minimize his pain, slam doors, and walk out, and Arthur knows that Brandon will complain and criticize. The fight grows predictable. Every defensive action Arthur takes in the fight makes him look even more uncaring to Brandon, and every defensive action Brandon takes makes him look more needy. Bad Reputations begin to develop and stick.

DEFENSE MODE BLOCKS ACCESS TO YOUR CORE

Defense Mode is like a callus on the skin—while the hard outer layer serves a protective function, it makes it more difficult to feel the softness underneath.

As defensive actions pile up, it becomes harder and harder for Brandon and Arthur to reach for a core way of expressing what they feel. Brandon no longer vocalizes the sensitive, calm, core version of what he feels—"I feel so sick and I really wish you could have been here with me earlier." He just complains and criticizes. Arthur no longer says, "I'm sorry. I had a tough day at work and needed a breather." He just turns his attention away from Brandon's needs. Stuck in Defense Mode, their actions get more antagonistic toward one another.

DEFENSE MODE BLINDS YOU TO YOUR PARTNER'S CORE

When they're entrenched in Defense Mode, it becomes almost impossible for Brandon and Arthur to see through that hard outer layer and remember that his partner has a good, kind, well-meaning, and vulnerable core in there, too. They no longer recall the specific threats that caused their partner to get defensive—they only see the defensive actions that they find irritating.

A POST-FIGHT FATAL ERROR

After each fight, Brandon and Arthur think about what just happened. Imagine if they could say to one another, "Wow, that got totally out of hand. We both lost it and acted in a way that was so out of character. I don't want to go through that again." The two would walk away with the perception that what happened during the fight was a crazy *exception* to their usual core selves, a momentary flip into Defense Mode that they can bounce back from.

On the other hand, if they stew on what their partner did during the fight and conclude that those actions are their partner's "true self," the fight will begin to harden into permanence. I call this the Defense–Core Error, in which you mistake your partner's Defense Mode Actions for his or her core self.

If Brandon ends up convinced that Arthur's behavior in the fight means that Arthur is a heartless tyrant who only cares about himself, and Arthur grows sure that Brandon is a needy hypochondriac who can never be satisfied, these labels become a permanent way of viewing who their partner is at the core. As they continue repeating those post-fight impressions to themselves over the ensuing months or years, the Defense–Core Error starts to seem more and more like truth. Negative views harden into Bad Reputations about the other person. They both feel absolutely sure that their partner has "changed" into a terrible version of his former self, and the fight settles into what I call Reputation Lock. Now they're really stuck.

When I meet with couples who are stuck in Reputation Lock, they often passionately describe just how terrible their partner has become. They almost can't believe how different their partner is now compared to how he or she was at the beginning of their relationship:

* "It's crazy, really, how someone's true colors come out after you've been together for a while!"
* "Doc, I'm telling you, she's the angriest person in the world. Can you believe this is what she screamed at me?
* "Well, he's the most cruel person you can imagine! Let me tell you what he actually said to me in that fight. . . . Who talks like that?"

REPUTATION LOCK

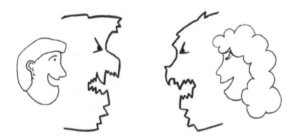

When I ask how they could possibly have ended up together in the first place if their partner is such a monster, they usually say something like, "somehow she concealed this from me," or "that must have been the honeymoon period—this is the *real* him."

To me, these kinds of Reputation Lock statements are like extreme versions of the Defense–Core Error. How the partner acts when in Defense Mode is interpreted as the authentic core of the partner, and that error eventually hardens into a Bad Reputation Fight.

THE TERRIBLE COSTS OF BEING IN REPUTATION LOCK

Couples in Reputation Lock feel constantly frustrated, and for good reason: The defensive actions that they use to try to protect themselves from pain instead keep them solidly in a state of suffering. Once they can recognize that they're stuck, though, they can work toward positive change.

EVERY ACTION ADDS TO THE BAD REPUTATION

Trapped in their respective Defense Modes, each partner's defensive behavior creates threats for the other, prompting reciprocal defensive behavior. All the bad behavior that exploded out of the argument from both sides is remembered, and it hardens to support the Bad Reputations that have been building. The more entrenched the Bad Reputations are, the more prone the couple is to have the conflict re-explode because of smaller and smaller triggers over time.

Brandon's efforts to feel closer to Arthur are interpreted as yet another clingy thing that "needy" Brandon is doing. Arthur's efforts to get some space from Brandon are interpreted as yet another dismissive thing that "uncaring" Arthur typically does.

When Arthur brings back a souvenir for Brandon from a business trip, Brandon doesn't think, "Wow, that was so nice." Instead, he sticks to the Bad Reputation he holds about Arthur and thinks: "I can tell he bought it in the airport at the last minute . . . he obviously gave it no thought at all. It shows once again that he doesn't care; he just rushed to get something out of obligation."

Of course, Arthur is no different. He, too, arrives on the scene with pessimistic expectations. Even as he offers Brandon the gift, he assumes that he'll get some kind of negative response. With Brandon's Bad Reputation clear in his mind, Arthur thinks, "He's so needy that nothing I do is ever enough for him. He'll just find some way to reject it."

Not surprisingly, the interaction turns out just as both expected. Arthur appears as uncaring as ever as he hands over the gift, and Brandon, as usual, seems impossible to please. Both walk away from the interaction believing that his partner's Bad Reputation is just and well deserved.

BOTH PARTNERS FEEL MISUNDERSTOOD AND THE BAD REPUTATIONS BECOME LOCKED

With locked mindsets, both partners talk about the other's Bad Reputation as if it's the truth, and both continue to try to change one another.

When Arthur says to Brandon, "You're so difficult to please . . . I wish you would stop being so needy," he hopes that this might encourage Brandon to

THE NEEDY
HYPOCHONDRIAC

change. But Brandon feels so deeply misjudged by this characterization, and so terribly hurt by it (it hits him like another threat), that he can do nothing else but respond defensively, reinforcing the same behavior that Arthur finds needy.

When Brandon says to Arthur, "You're such an uncaring partner; I wish you would actually show some compassion sometimes," he hopes this might encourage Arthur to change. But Arthur also feels misjudged by this description—he

THE UNCARING, SELFISH
PARTNER

doesn't perceive himself to be uncaring—and that hurts (another threat), so he reacts with anger and distance. Both Arthur and Brandon feel outraged about how the other sees him and feel locked in by the other's frame.

If you asked each of them, "Brandon, are you really needy and difficult to please?" or "Arthur, are you really uncaring about Brandon?" both would reject those characterizations. Brandon might say, "I only seem needy because I'm so starved for any attention from Arthur. If he cared about me like a normal partner, I wouldn't be the least bit needy!" Arthur, on the other hand, might explain, "I only seem uncaring because Brandon's standard is ridiculous—who could possibly meet his expectations?"

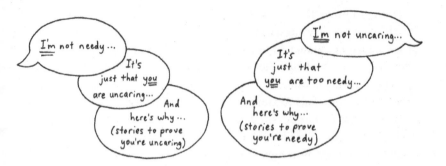

They each believe that their partner is to blame for the overall problem between them. They both wish the other would drop his insistence on these mistaken Bad Reputations and see the truth; they can't change how they're seen and it's intensely frustrating.

PARTNERS SET UP TESTS TO PROVE BAD REPUTATIONS

When couples are stuck in Reputation Lock, they often try to prove that their characterization of their partner is right by consciously or subconsciously setting up tests for one another. When the partner predictably fails the test, there's a sense of vindication: "You see? I was right about you!"

Trying to prove that a Bad Reputation is deserved is usually dangerous. People often say they engage in tests like this to "give my partner a chance to prove me wrong, so then I can change my opinion of him." But because tests often end with a "Gotcha!" the partner being tested inevitably feels he was set up to fail, proving nothing.

When Brandon fails Arthur's test at the party, he walks away feeling even more sure that Arthur doesn't care about him—why would a caring partner deliberately ignore him like that at a party? When Arthur fails Brandon's lab-results test, he walks away more convinced that Brandon is needy—only a really needy person would be so sensitive about what questions you do or don't ask! As we can see, putting your Reputation-Locked view of your partner to the test only adds iron bolts to their Reputation-Locked view of you. The lock tightens and the enmity for one another grows.

BREAKING THE REPUTATION LOCK

Clients often ask me, "Do you really think people can change? Aren't personalities pretty fixed by a certain age?" Interestingly, the question is usually presented in this form:

> S/He is so...
>
> immature   boring
> clingy   disinterested   messy
> obsessive   withholding
> critical   lazy   unemotional   explosive
> workaholic
>
> (pick annoying personality trait)
> How likely is it that s/he can change?

Couples ask this partly as a way to decide whether they should invest in working on a relationship where they feel stuck. "If my partner is never going to be any different, then why should I bother working on the relationship?" or "When I start to see my partner act a little less (insert annoying personality trait), then I'll be willing to work on our relationship."

When couples say these kinds of things, I feel inclined to ask a different question: "How likely is it that *you* could change *your view* of your partner as so (insert annoying personality trait)?" It may not seem obvious at first, but *your view* of your partner, especially that locked Bad Reputation you've placed on him or her, makes it more difficult for your partner to change.

Wait, this seems very confusing. You may be asking, "How can what *I* think about another person *prevent him or her* from changing?"

Recall from the Nagging-Tuning Out Fight in Chapter 3, how thoughts and judgments influence actions. What you think about your partner's characteristics drives how you act toward them, which can inadvertently reinforce exactly those behaviors you want your partner to change.

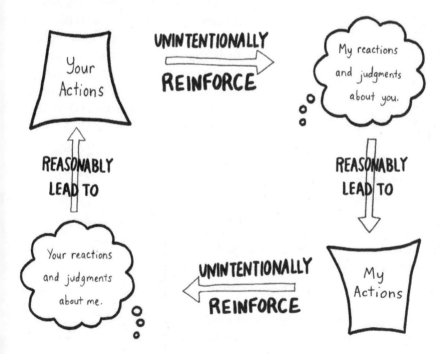

To stop a cycle like this, you have to consider not just changing the *actions* you take, but the *thoughts* you have. Here's why: People tend to behave well when they're around people who they believe value them and see them positively. In contrast, in environments where a person doesn't feel valued or well liked, he or she tends to behave less well because, well, what's the point?

For example, when Raj's boss tells him that he has the most potential of any worker on the team, Raj's performance will likely improve even more. Why does this happen? Is it simply a self-fulfilling prophecy? Not really—human behavior tends to be somewhat predictable on this point. The more a person feels that he or she is making a positive impression, the more that person feels motivated to show his or her positive capabilities. When you find

yourself in an environment that encourages you, that sees the worth in your efforts, and that tolerates your unintentional mistakes, you feel more internally motivated to continue working at difficult challenges.

This works in the opposite direction, too. An employee—let's call him Dillon—suspects that his boss doubts his abilities. He finds himself becoming increasingly cautious, taking less initiative, and sometimes even making more mistakes. Is Dillon's lack of success because he feels demoralized? Quite likely. In addition, Dillon has

to expend a lot of energy worrying about how the boss will react to his work, while Raj feels more secure to take chances, knowing that the boss will have his back. In other words, the more frequently you find yourself in an environment that views you in a negative light, the more difficult it is to perform at your best.

In couples, labels can operate in much the same way. People tend not to consider how, by tightly holding on to a negative reputation about a partner, they're inadvertently reinforcing it. In fact, many people find this point to be counterintuitive or hard to accept. "After all," they say, "my partner *deserves* that Bad Reputation, because he or she acts in a way that reinforces it." It's certainly more instinctual to hold people responsible for their own faults and to see faults as intrinsic to the person rather than as very influenced by that person's environment. But it's that instinct that keeps people stuck. Holding a partner in Reputation Lock creates an incredibly strong critical environment, which makes change even more difficult for the partner. It turns out that the question, "Can people change?" should really be, "Under what conditions can people change?"

The good news is that once you understand the role that reputations play in affecting behavior, you can find options to help your partner actually change by adjusting the messages he or she hears from you and releasing him or her from the Reputation Lock.

Here's an example of Reputation Lock that I witnessed in my practice: Sheryl announced, "Jonah isn't very loving anymore. He never says, 'I love you' or greets me with a kiss. I'm tired of living without affection." Later in that same session, Jonah talked about a weekend he spent away from Sheryl, with friends. He got a bit choked up. With a tender expression and tears in his eyes, he said to Sheryl, "I missed you so much. It made me remember just how much I love you." At that moment, Sheryl looked away. I asked, "Sheryl, what do you make of that?" to give her an opportunity to respond in some warm way to Jonah's heartfelt expression of affection. Instead, Sheryl answered, "He says that now, but when we leave this office will he say it again? I doubt it."

Sheryl didn't respond to Jonah's expression of love or even show that it affected her positively. She communicated that it wasn't enough and returned to insisting that he was the uncaring person she knew him to be. Of course, Sheryl had her reasons for responding in this way—for years she needed to protect herself from hoping to get more from Jonah and being repeatedly disappointed. As a result, it's hard for her to believe that he could be different than his longstanding Bad Reputation. But for Jonah, when he *is* loving and then sees her insist that he isn't, he feels locked back into the "uncaring" label he's been trying to escape for years. Feeling slighted, Jonah isn't likely to risk offering more loving expressions. Instead, he'll probably respond in a way that distances himself from this interaction, and Sheryl will have even more evidence that he doesn't show any affection.

Because Reputation Locks make change in a relationship incredibly difficult, it can help to deliberately create an encouraging environment with your partner. If Sheryl welcomed and appreciated each little step Jonah took in the direction of expressing affection, he'd be more encouraged to take additional risks. By letting go of the Reputation Lock she has of him being "uncaring," she does her part to make change more likely. Of course, it's not only up to Sheryl to change her mindset. Jonah has his own work to do, which includes challenging *his* locked assumption that nothing he does for Sheryl will ever be enough.

STOPPING THE BAD REPUTATION FIGHT

As we've seen, Reputation Locks develop when partners repeatedly make the Defense–Core Error: They keep interpreting the Defense Mode behaviors they see as integral parts of their partner's core, rather than just automatic responses to threat. They start to view their partner only in light of this negative reputation and no longer recognize the positive attributes of their partner's core that attracted them in the first place. To avoid the Defense–Core Error and to break the Reputation Lock, both partners must challenge and change the way they think about one another.

CHOOSE TO BELIEVE IN THE CORE, NOT THE BAD REPUTATION

Who is your partner? The person you get when he's defending himself from threats? Or the person who exists at his core? Under the Defense Mode Actions and the Bad Reputation lives your partner's positive core self, but in a threat-filled environment, the Defense Mode version of him is all you see. To peel off those defensive layers and mistaken assumptions to get back to the core, you have to break the frame you've got your partner locked into. In the case of Brandon and Arthur, Brandon isn't really a needy hypochondriac; he is a person who feels out of touch with his partner. Arthur isn't an uncaring brute; he's feeling crowded and is longing for some freedom.

THE NEEDY
HYPOCHONDRIAC

THE UNCARING, SELFISH
PARTNER

It isn't easy to suddenly break the frame you have about your partner, but there is often a built-in motivator to do so: Reputation Locked frames usually come in pairs, with both partners misreading each other. Since you know that your partner is wrong in his or her thinking about you, you might be ready to consider that you are wrong about your partner, too.

TAKE RESPONSIBILITY FOR YOUR CONTRIBUTIONS

We can all acknowledge that when a partner accuses us of being a certain way, there's generally at least a little kernel of truth to it. "You're such a control freak," is usually directed at a partner who likes to be in charge more than most. "You're so inconsiderate," is leveled at a person who isn't particularly attentive to details. A Bad Reputation rarely forms out of the clear blue sky.

If you own up to and take responsibility for your typical defensive pattern, you can help shed the heavier Bad Reputation. For example, you might say something like, "I know that you see me as controlling/inconsiderate/(other negative label), and I know that I *do* act that way sometimes, so I get why you think that. But I want to try harder not to be so controlling/inconsiderate/ (other negative label). And I know you hate it when I call you lazy/withholding/(other negative label). Let's put down these Bad Reputation weapons and talk about the feelings that brought us to this point instead. I *know* you're so much more than what I've called you in the past."

FIND THE THREATS

Try to look for and understand the specific threats that repeatedly result in Defense Mode and may harden into Reputation Lock. Use the Repairing Conversations steps from the Birthday Fight in Chapter 6 to examine each part of the cycle that's causing the fight. Pause your defensive actions, locate the threats you unintentionally put out, and discuss them with your partner. After both partners understand the fight cycle, a change in mindset becomes possible.

Brandon acts in a clingy way when he feels abandoned or not cared about. That's not his whole personality. He wouldn't be clingy if he didn't feel the threat of losing my caring. What he really needs is to be reassured that I care.

Loss of caring from Arthur

STOP THE PAIN: Get him to care by showing more need

Arthur does care about me, but he starts to distance himself from me when he feels threatened that I'm judging him. He's not uncaring at heart; that's just him in Defense Mode. If I help him not feel judged he probably won't be as distant.

GET SOME FREEDOM

Take space for self, minimize Brandon's needs

Smothered / overwhelmed by Brandon's needs

Notice that both Arthur and Brandon are interpreting one another's behavior as a complex response to threats and as a mutual dynamic, not as a fixed quality of their partner's personality. They stop boxing one another into locked Bad Reputations and start seeing one another's behaviors as Defense Mode Actions that happen only when their partner feels threatened. These actions aren't coming from their core; they're not reflective of who their partner truly is, so holding on to those old reputations doesn't make sense. Best of all, once they begin *thinking* this way, they can begin *communicating* differently.

As each partner relieves the other of a previously launched threat, both find it easier to drop their Defense Modes. The interaction starts to spiral in a positive direction toward more supportive communication. Over time, the Bad Reputations will soften and fade into a more nuanced understanding of one another.

A POSTSCRIPT ABOUT REPUTATION LOCK

Occasionally I'll work with a couple where one partner, or both, absolutely refuses to drop the Bad Reputations they hold about the other and consider any alternative way to see their partner.

"He's an egomaniac. That's it, and nothing is going to change"

"She's just a boring person . . . she has never wanted to do anything fun."

"He'll never take initiative—even his boss complains about it."

"She's explosive and angry and she'll never be able to control it."

When I propose widening their perspective to see what core might be hiding under their partner's thick Defense Mode layer—the egotistical, dull, passive, or explosive (etc.) behavior—they insist that no such good core exists. "Sorry, Doc, you don't know her like I know her. There's *no* good in there!"

In situations where the Defense–Core Error and Reputation Lock are this deeply embedded, you *can* reach a point of no return. And it's understandable. Couples at that extreme are in so much pain that it's often irresistible to go for the small relief that comes with labeling the other person as the problem. But, once you permanently feel so much resentment toward your partner and are engaged in a tight Reputation Lock, it's nearly impossible to create a better relationship.

So yes, some Reputation Locks do get too locked to unlock. But before you assume that you and your partner are Reputation-Locked beyond repair, make an effort to find your partner's core, even if it's completely obscured by defenses. With small advances into Core Mode you can reset your interactions with one another from constant Defense Mode and start loosening the lock.

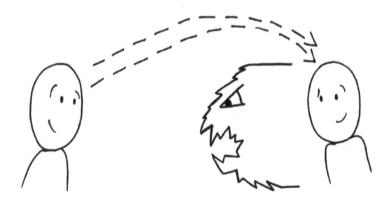

THE BAD REPUTATION FIGHT TOOLBOX

 Don't mistake your partner's Defense Mode Actions for who he or she really is at the core.

 Avoid setting up "tests" that reinforce Reputation-Locked, negative labels of your partner.

 Be willing to challenge your assumptions about your partner.

 Understand the connection between the threats your partner feels and his or her Defense Mode Actions.

 Look behind the Bad Reputation that you have formed about your partner and seek a connection to who he or she truly is.

REPUTATION LOCK

CHAPTER 8

THE "YOU DON'T CARE ABOUT ME" FIGHT

MY PRIORITIES

1. Work
2. Kids & Dog
3. Exercise
4. Friends
5. Favorite Shows
   ooking
   lding
   he News
   edia
   rties

711. EVERYTHING ELSE IMAGINABLE
712. MY PARTNER

STEVE HAS ALWAYS BEEN A bit disorganized with schedules. Time gets away from him at the office and it's hard for him to predict when he'll leave work. When Marla calls to ask what time he'll be home, he usually tells her 6:30 in the evening but then routinely doesn't show up until 7:30, which is very frustrating for her. She's often requested that he just tell her "the real time" he'll arrive rather than "the time he wishes" so that she can plan accordingly. But he frequently forgets (or blows through) whatever time estimate he makes. It drives Marla nuts!

Notice how Marla interprets Steve's behavior:

* "You don't care!"
* "You're disrespecting me!"
* "You do it on purpose!"

Marla's reaction is understandable; she's told Steve that his lateness is annoying over and over, but for some reason he keeps doing it. In her eyes, he *knows* how important being on time is to her, so why does he ignore her repeated request? She begins to believe that his behavior means something worse—it seems deliberately uncaring and disrespectful. Because she's been frustrated by his lateness so many times, she has labeled him with a Bad Reputation of being uncaring and disrespectful. As a result, Steve's explanations for his behavior are completely unconvincing to Marla.

Steve feels frustrated, too. He can't stand it when Marla labels his actions as uncaring. In his eyes, she just doesn't understand the pressure he's under at work and that he does strive to be home with his family as quickly as he can. If he really didn't care, as she assumes, he'd actually be home much later! But she doesn't give him any credit for working as hard as he does to make it home for dinner. Sure, sometimes he's later than he expects, but it has nothing to do with how he feels about Marla, so why can't she cut him some slack? It's especially frustrating to be called uncaring when he actually does care about her a lot. But she won't believe him, and that upsets him.

Steve's reaction is understandable; he feels unfairly accused. To him, a small thing is being blown up into a huge transgression. It's as if Marla thinks she knows why he was late better than he does, which is infuriating! They get stuck arguing about whether Steve does or does not care about Marla, with Steve insisting that he does and Marla declaring that he must not—if he did, he'd *show it* by being home on time. The fight about coming home on time turns into the "You Don't Care About Me" Fight.

THE FIGHT OF ALL FIGHTS

The "You Don't Care About Me" Fight could be called the Fight of All Fights since arguments about other subjects often spiral into a fight about caring. The reason for this is simple: Almost anything a couple argues about can trigger worries about the amount of caring in a relationship.

Consider the fights we've discussed so far. In all Partner Improvement Fights (see Chapter 1), if your efforts to change your partner land on deaf ears, you can easily interpret his or her unwillingness to change as a result of uncaring. Marla's wish for Steve's improvement in time management is an example of this. In the Bad Reputation Fight (see Chapter 7), Brandon senses that Arthur has stopped caring for him because he doesn't tend to him when he's sick. In the Proving Your Point Fight (see Chapter 2), the fact that Teresa can't provide Charles with a calm environment when he comes home feels uncaring to him, and the fact that Charles doesn't appreciate Teresa's efforts for the family feels uncaring to her. As the Escalating Fight (see Chapter 4) heats up, the awful things that are said leave both partners with the feeling that those insults came from an uncaring heart, and not getting enough help with the household chores makes Jeanette feel uncared about (see Chapter 5).

The "uncaring" theme runs across virtually all fights, as you'll continue to see in the coming chapters. Fights about money, sex, and whether you prioritize family members over your partner can all kick off the "You Don't Care About Me" Fight. Any conflict, no matter how big or small, can leave both parties feeling that the other person doesn't care enough.

IT'S ALL ABOUT CARING

Why can almost any fight boil down to a tension about whether a partner cares or not? It's because caring is a most elemental part of a relationship. While there are many things people desire with an intimate partner, like great sex, good conversation, laughs, and doing other enjoyable things together, at the heart of it all, what makes a relationship feel genuinely bonded is the sense that your partner truly cares about you. The sex, the conversation, the laughs, and the activities together all seem much better if the partner you're sharing them with also cares about you. And ongoing care and respect feels like love.

When a partner does something that appears to communicate a *lack* of caring, it can change how you feel about the relationship. You got a big raise and your partner forgets to say congratulations. You break your ankle and your partner doesn't realize how hard it is for you to get around. You're excited about a car you really want and your partner won't even consider looking at it. You do something super thoughtful and your partner doesn't notice. You speak and your partner doesn't listen. Just as all humans respond in certain ways to social threats, we also all long for some sense of care that comes with an intimate relationship. Here's the variety of kinds of caring that we want:

WAYS OF CARING

YOU ARE AVAILABLE, PRESENT FOR ME

YOU'RE SUPPORTIVE WHEN I'M WEAK

YOU MOURN MY FAILURES WITH ME

YOU CHEER FOR MY SUCCESS

YOU LOVE ME EVEN THOUGH I AM NOT PERFECT

YOU WANT ME

YOU COMFORT AND HOLD ME

YOUR LOVE IS VISIBLE IN YOUR BODY, YOUR WORDS, AND YOUR ACTIONS

WHEN I NEED YOU, YOU RESPOND

YOU KNOW WHO I REALLY AM

Relationships in which both partners demonstrate many of these ways of showing care feel most satisfying and are therefore more likely to last for the long haul. We count on our partners for validation, support, appreciation, and most of all, connection. When it isn't there, we get rattled. Truly feeling that connection to your partner forms the glue of a good relationship; if we feel cared about, we feel secure. With the comfort of a stable and secure partner, we can take risks out in the world. If we don't have the security of a loving, caring base, it becomes painfully unbalancing. So we're set up for what might be the most painful threat of all: loss of caring.

Universally, loss of caring from a partner hurts. While some people are more sensitive or feel it sooner than others, it's human nature to have some pained reaction when you perceive a partner distancing him- or herself or becoming less caring. When it happens, we don't like it one bit. The feeling that the person who is supposed to love you the most *doesn't* is so awful, it's no wonder we feel uneasy at the first sign of it.

Doubts and concerns about a partner's level of interest and affection are threats that can send anyone into Defense Mode, so it's understandable why Marla interprets Steve's behavior the way she does—she's worried.

Finding yourself on the receiving end of the "You Don't Care!" accusation, though, is also threatening. Being told that you don't care can arouse feelings such as, "Who are you to tell me what I'm thinking?" or "You're just misinterpreting me, and you are way off base!" Unfairly, once your partner starts to believe that you're uncaring, *anything* you do can get labeled as yet another piece of evidence that "You Don't Care!"

No one likes it when a partner thinks he or she can mind-read every one of your actual intentions and feelings simply from your behavior. Steve feels outraged that Marla believes she really knows why he's late, and he hates how she interprets his actions. Feeling falsely accused of not caring creates a threat that can also send someone into Defense Mode, which is precisely what happens to Steve.

So here's how the "You Don't Care About Me" Fight looks from the standpoint of Marla's and Steve's respective threats, and the Defense Mode Actions that those threats stimulate:

Once the "You Don't Care About Me" Fight gets going, *both* partners begin to feel uncared for—Marla because of Steve's repeated lateness, but now Steve, too, because he's being falsely accused. Under that threat, Steve may ultimately decide to fight back.

Of course, Steve's angry retort (his Defense Mode Action) becomes yet another threat to Marla, and she's likely to pull out another one of her own Defense Mode Actions—perhaps explaining emphatically and angrily why he deserves to be yelled at and accused. Round and round they go, spiraling further and further into the "You Don't Care About Me" Fight vortex.

STOPPING THE "YOU DON'T CARE ABOUT ME" FIGHT

The "You Don't Care About Me" Fight is driven by two main factors: misinterpretation (from Marla's side) and a lack of attention to the impact of actions (from Steve's side). Let's explore these two triggers one at a time.

MISINTERPRETATION

Marla interprets Steve's behavior in a way that he just can't agree with—Steve knows he wasn't intentionally "uncaring" when he came home late, so he rejects Marla's label outright.

Once her interpretation (or, rather, misinterpretation) of Steve's actions is attached, his reputation with her is no longer just, "he's always disorganized." It's now, "he's uncaring and disrespectful," which is a far more negative reputation.

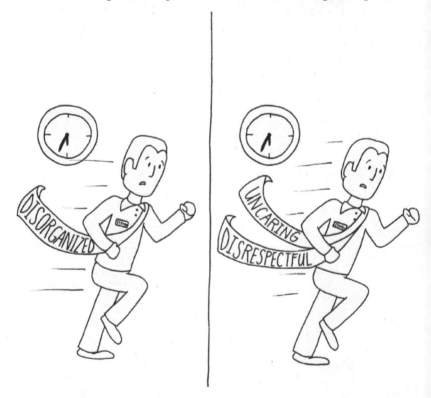

For Steve, being labeled as disorganized is something he could probably *agree* with and might even apologize for! He might even be willing to constructively fix it by acknowledging his tendency to be late and therefore tell Marla he'll be home an hour later than he actually expects. But being labeled as uncaring and disrespectful? That is *not* OK. Those words hit him like a threat. He won't accept these labels as simple feedback from Marla; no, they're an insult, a threat that bumps him into Defense Mode. So out come his shield and sword—he's going to fight her in order to prove that she's wrong about him.

In an interesting way, when Marla adds this extra, negative meaning to Steve's behavior, it affects her badly, too. Putting up with someone else's disorganized behavior is a challenge and very annoying, but if you have to put up with someone disrespecting you, that makes you feel like a doormat. As soon as Marla calls Steve's behavior "uncaring and disrespectful," she suffers from the threat that results.

Once coming home late is considered uncaring and disrespectful, if Steve does it again, she has to consider herself disrespected. That's enough to make anyone irate! Out come her defenses.

Now Marla is in a tighter bind. Steve is likely to continue to fail at getting home on time (simply because disorganized people don't often suddenly get good at time management) and each time she'll feel more disrespected. The stakes have grown higher for each of them. If Steve messes up and gets home after he said he would, he's got to worry that it supports Marla's incorrect view of him—which is exactly what he so desperately wants to disprove.

If only the stakes weren't so high. If only coming home late could go back to being just about Steve being disorganized. It would free them both. When I propose that to some couples, I sometimes get this reaction:

The stakes SHOULD be high! Maybe if he realizes how bad it is when he gets home late, he won't do it as much.

Marla believes it *helps* to keep labeling his behavior as "You Don't Care About Me" because she hopes raising the stakes will encourage him to be less disorganized and late. But when she makes it more risky to be late, does it prod Steve into becoming more organized about time? Actually, no. And that's fairly typical. In situations where people sense that they'll get *more* grief from a partner, they sometimes paradoxically try to improve less! Sometimes it comes down to this:

> I have absolutely no chance of changing Marla's mind about me when it comes to being late. If I come home on time I'll get no credit. She only focuses on when I'm late and then makes a huge deal. Why bother trying?

STEPHEN'S TRACK RECORD	
Comes Home On Time	Comes Home Late
NO CREDIT	
	YELLED AT
	SCREAMED AT
	SCOWLED AT
NO CREDIT	
	NAG-A-THON
NO CREDIT	

Unfortunately, Marla's strategy to get Steve to come home on time by raising the stakes backfires.

LACK OF ATTENTION TO IMPACT

Marla isn't the only one contributing to this fight, though. Steve is responsible for his side of it, too. The fact is, Steve *is* often late—to meetings, to social events, and when coming home in the evenings. This behavior isn't specific to how he feels about Marla, but it sure feels that way to her. Maybe he doesn't care if he inconveniences coworkers, but she feels he *should* care about inconveniencing his family.

On some level, Steve knows that he isn't good at time management, though he doesn't like to admit it. It's actually a problem for him at work, too, and one that might not easily go away, even if he works at it. Habits are hard to break, after all. Of course, Steve's behavior has an impact on Marla and makes her tremendously frustrated.

But Steve doesn't easily acknowledge that. He just talks about his good intentions and minimizes the bad effects of his actions. This lack of attention to impact is the second engine that drives the "You Don't Care About Me" Fight.

As we saw before in the Proving Your Point Fight (see Chapter 2), intent and impact matter a lot in a conflict. As long as Steve focuses on proving his good intentions and Marla focuses on proving the bad impact of his actions, the fight cycle is doomed to continue. Even though it sounds like their points of view are completely at odds, actually both of their statements are true. Steve's intentions *are* good—he's working as hard as he can and juggling a lot, but it's also true that his actions have an unintended bad impact on Marla.

When each partner talks only about his or her side of the dynamic between them, they argue. It's when Steve acknowledges his own bad impact and Marla realizes Steve's good intent that the fight begins to unravel. Here's how it might look:

Notice a few important elements of this exchange.

First, Steve admits to his problem. He doesn't claim that it didn't happen, or that Marla is making a big deal about nothing. This is important. If you're someone with a habit that irritates others, you can do a lot for your relationships simply by acknowledging that you know it's a problem. Admitting that the habit has a negative impact on your partner and that it's something you also *want* to change shows empathy for your partner's dilemma and provides him or her with the comfort of knowing that you see the problem, too. Denying the problem usually just compels your partner to complain about your bad impact yet again!

Second, Marla shows she's aware of Steve's good intentions and reinforces that by thanking him for his empathy toward her. Next, is what she *doesn't* do. She doesn't make suggestions or give advice about how Steve should solve the problem. She lets him think about it and stay in control of solving his time management problem. That provides him with even more space to take responsibility for it.

Paying attention to and understanding the impact that your less-than-desirable habits have on your partner and taking ownership over working to fix them will lead your partner to feel less need to remind or nag you about them. In addition, even if you still struggle with changing the negative habit, the fact that you're trying to do something about it makes it much less likely that any difficulty you encounter in changing the habit will be interpreted as a sign of uncaring. As an imperfect human being, you may not always get it right, but your partner will know you care enough to work on it. That right there can put a stop to the "You Don't Care About Me" Fight.

If it turns out that Steve is a bit oblivious to his impact and unable to begin this dialogue, then Marla can start it by correcting her half of the "You Don't Care About Me" Fight. She can make sure to avoid interpreting his lateness as a sign of uncaring and instead lead their conversation off with a mention of Steve's good intentions:

With this less critical approach, Steve is much more open to accepting his responsibility for the problem. Here, Marla shows empathy for the challenges Steve faces, appreciates his efforts even when he isn't always successful, and stays on his side to help find a solution that works for both of them. His tardiness is still annoying, but she's deliberate about how she interprets his behavior and is careful not to affix any additional meaning to it. She knows that it doesn't mean he doesn't care about her. Notice that when Marla gives Steve the benefit of the doubt about his intentions, she also relays back to him that she knows his bad impact was unintentional. As long as she opens her feedback with mention of his good intentions, he's likely to be receptive to hearing about his bad impact.

You might be thinking, "Sure, that could work if that was the first time it happened, but what if Marla already had a Reputation Lock on Steve and couldn't bring herself to believe that his being late was just about being late?" This is true: Breaking the Reputation Lock requires a watershed conversation— one that deliberately declares an end to an old assumption.

As with any Locked Reputation, though, it's not going to be easy for Marla to suddenly consider that she was wrong about her interpretation of Steve's behavior (or for Steve to understand that Marla's frustration is about something much more significant than lateness). It can takes many rounds of the "You Don't Care About Me" Fight for one of the partners to stop and ask, "What am I missing about what's going on here?" and open up a possibility for the lock to be undone. Sometimes it requires having a couples therapist take a close look at the knot between a couple to help them see that an assumption-changing conversation needs to happen.

Such a conversation might not even instantly resolve the fight or the Reputation Lock (see Chapter 7), but it does open up a new beginning so that going forward they can work from both sides to prevent the fight. Marla can commit to not misinterpreting Steve's actions, and Steve can commit to being more aware of the bad impact he's been having and to take on responsibility for working on his lateness.

"YOU DON'T CARE ABOUT ME" FIGHTS AND DEFENSE MODE

In the case of Marla and Steve, Steve's difficulty in predicting when he'd come home triggered a "You Don't Care About Me" response from Marla. But once their fight really got going, Marla's accusation prompted Steve to throw it back at her:

Steve feels the sting of Marla's Defense Mode reaction (her accusation), which seems uncaring to him. In fact, you can begin to see that *any* Defense Mode Actions can send a couple straight into the "You Don't Care About Me" Fight, since those actions can be interpreted as a threat of the lack of caring. Consider the wide variety of Defense Mode behaviors that people use to respond to a threat from their partner:

Defensive behaviors always make some emotional sense because they move people away from threats. The problem, though, is that these behaviors can easily come across as non-caring. Some people leave the room in the middle of a fight because high-octane conflict feels very threatening. But leaving the room makes their partner go ballistic because, "How could a caring partner walk out on me?!" Stating a point louder and stronger may make sense under the threat of being dismissed, but for the receiving partner, "If you cared, you would never yell at me!"

Among the huge variety of defensive actions that people call upon in response to a threat, everyone has their favorites. Some always fight: yelling, striking back with harsh criticism, or hurling insults. Others prefer flight: They avoid their partner by staying late at work, or only focusing on the kids, or by never lifting their eyes from their phone, or maybe they go with the silent treatment. For others, their Defense Mode Actions are about soothing themselves by overspending, drinking, or getting lost in porn. Each of these strategies serves the same purpose: to lessen the pain of an incoming threat. But they *all* can be interpreted by a partner as signals that you don't care.

This man is trying to cool the fight down by separating himself from his partner, which, in some ways could be seen as quite caring, because he's striving for *less* conflict. But because his partner perceives the distance he creates as ignoring her, she feels a loss of caring from him and is likely to go into Defense

Mode herself. Once both partners are in Defense Mode, no matter their choice of defensive action, the fight begins to look like this:

Each partner feels that the other doesn't care enough because each has experienced behavior from the other that feels uncaring. Not feeling cared about makes both of them feel desperate, scared, unhappy, and alone, so they each react with their own particular Defense Mode Actions. The cycle continues as they keep triggering one another, and now the "You Don't Care About Me" Fight is aflame.

Sometimes couples in my office argue about whose Defense Mode Actions are more uncaring and therefore are more to blame for the fights they have. "Isn't it worse to yell the way she does? I'm calm and quiet, and she's the one who goes crazy!" Or, "I'm just trying to get things out the open. Isn't that better than sweeping everything under the rug and avoiding it?"

Here's how I answer: If whatever you're doing launches a threat toward your partner, it's contributing to the fight. If the way you're "calm and quiet" during a fight causes your partner to feel abandoned (and uncared for), it's not simply "calm and quiet." If the way you "get things out in the open" causes your partner to feel attacked (and uncared for), it's not simply "being open." It isn't worth splitting hairs over whose version of bad behavior is worse when the Defense Mode Actions of *both* sides keep the pain going for everyone. The key is to understand this cycle of mutual uncaring and be able to take action against it *together*.

Another way to think about the "You Don't Care About Me" Fight is as a very common form of Defense–Core Error.

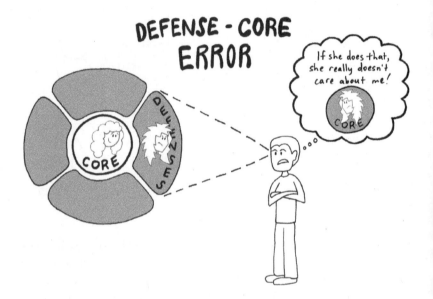

DEFENSE - CORE ERROR

If she does that, she really doesn't care about me!

It's in our basic human nature to want all the elements of caring: to be recognized, responded to, visibly loved, comforted, desired, cherished, and supported. Therefore, any defensive act from a partner that demonstrates a failure to provide those needs can get summarized as, "At the core, my partner doesn't care about me." We don't stop to distinguish Defense Mode Actions from what a partner might really feel at the core. What we see during a conflict morphs into what we believe are our partner's "true colors." Making this error keeps us firmly stuck in "You Don't Care About Me" Fights.

Let's be honest, though. When you feel threatened and enter Defense Mode in the heat of a battle, you *do* temporarily stop caring about the impact you have. You go for the jugular, and you say what is most hurtful or what will intentionally provoke your partner. You don't care if shouting or distancing yourself hurts the other person; you do it anyway. It's the nature of Defense Mode behavior to depart from your civilized, core self. When you go into animal-like survival mode against threats, you do whatever it takes to feel safe. You don't pay attention to your partner's feelings because *you actually don't care* while in the heat of the moment.

In that moment of fury with one another, it's as if both partners are saying, "I want to make you feel as much hurt as I feel!"

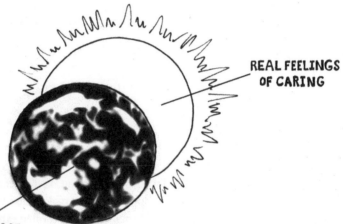

REAL FEELINGS
OF CARING

TEMPORARY BURST
OF DEFENSE MODE

The caring gets eclipsed by the fight.

* "I don't care if walking out hurts you—I'm so hurt I don't care about you!"
* "I don't care if calling you a jerk hurts you—you deserve it!"
* "I don't care if overspending will bother you—I'm so hurt I'm doing it anyway!"
* "I don't care if staying out late with my friends annoys you—it feels terrible to be around you!"

People don't typically want to admit that "yes, temporarily, I did stop caring about you when I was so fired up," but it's what we do. Defense Mode clouds your vision and your judgment. It pulls you away from living according to your values, and even from what you feel very deeply at your core. Take the case of Ray and Tami, for example:

How can Ray reconcile that Tami says "I love you" in a quiet moment and "I hate your guts!" during a fight? It doesn't seem to make sense that one person could feel such opposite things about someone. So, Ray often explains it to himself by thinking, "What was said in the *fight* must be the truth because that's when she wasn't holding back. She really doesn't care about me." If Ray understands that "I hate your guts" comes when Tami is fighting off perceived threats but that it doesn't come from her core, he can avoid making the Defense–Core Error and instead understand, "Tami does care about me, but when she feels threatened she expresses the opposite." Hanging on to the assumption that caring *is* there, underneath the battle, actually gives you more leverage to *stop* future fights.

Sometimes I'll say to a client, "Your partner really does care about you at the core level, but it's hard to see that when she's in Defense Mode," and he'll push back with, "No, if she really cared about me, she'd be able to better control her reactions. If she 'loses it,' how can I believe there's anything different under there?" And it is certainly very hard. But we can learn something about assumptions of caring from a different sort of relationship situation: parenting.

A loving parent sometimes "loses it" and yells at his kids in a moment of frustration. We can recognize that the outburst doesn't mean that he doesn't have deep love for his kids. Somehow we sort the behavior into two boxes—the more consistent loving relationship and the occasional outburst when the situation becomes too frustrating. It's the same for couples, except we tend to be less forgiving and less willing to sort the behavior in that manner. But if you're able to see it that way, it can greatly calm the fear of not being cared about. You can try having a Repairing Conversation that helps with the sorting:

For the relationship to truly be repaired, after this conversation Tami will need to keep showing Ray more of her loving side, reassuring him that the "I hate you" behavior is a rare exception. And though it may be hard, Ray will have to at least tentatively trust Tami's explanation in their Repairing Conversation and not hold on to his view that "she's uncaring through-and-through."

In short, the "You Don't Care About Me" Fight is driven by a universally awful feeling that the bond we have with a partner is loosening or breaking. Drifting or blasting apart, the feeling of greater and greater distance between partners makes each of them feel terribly alone. When one partner says, "You don't care about me!" the message from the core is really something like, "I'm worried about our relationship. I wish we could be closer and more loving, but I feel this distance growing between us. I wish it wasn't there. Can we figure out a way to be closer again?"

When a partner says, "You don't care about me!" he or she is frightened and looking for reassurance, hoping the response will be, "Don't worry—of course I care about you!" But a quick, superficial reassurance isn't enough to make that fear go away. Feeling fully connected again takes real Core-to-Core Communication.

Emotional distance can be bridged by verbalizing to your partner what you long for and what you fear: "I feel distant from you and want to reconnect," or "I fear that you don't love me anymore and I don't know what to do to feel closer again." When you speak from the core, it's much easier for a partner to respond from the core as well: "I feel distant, too . . . let's find a way to reconnect." This is the true fix for the "You Don't Care About Me" Fight—a conversation that rebuilds your connection and a joint recommitment to make an effort to show one another love through the many "Ways of Caring."

THE "YOU DON'T CARE ABOUT ME" FIGHT TOOLBOX

 Recognize the threats that underlie the fight and seek to soothe the threats your partner feels.

 Stop the two main drivers of the "You Don't Care About Me" Fight: misinterpretation and not paying enough attention to bad impact.

 Don't automatically label non-perfect behavior as "uncaring."

 Take responsibility for your own non-perfect behavior and the bad impact it has on your partner.

 Remember that all Defense Mode Actions can eclipse real caring. Work together to stay out of Defense Mode and keep the caring visible.

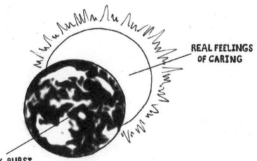

REAL FEELINGS OF CARING

TEMPORARY BURST OF DEFENSE MODE

CHAPTER 9

THE PARENTING DIFFERENCES FIGHT

HUGH **AND CHONDRA HAVE TWO** children, ages eight and six. As a couple, they find themselves constantly arguing about how to raise their children. Hugh loves the outdoors and wants to share his love of camping, hiking, and skiing with his kids. He finds it so frustrating that every time he suggests doing one of these activities, Chondra puts up some resistance, complaining that it's just not safe enough. It seems to Hugh that Chondra would rather they not do anything fun if there's even a remote chance that they'll be bitten by an insect, get a splinter, or be out after dark.

> It's like she wants them to grow up in a bubble! Her fears are totally out of proportion and she is obsessed with organic food.
>
> We ate hot dogs and fried chicken as kids, and we made it to adulthood.

Hugh believes that giving their children broad life experiences is very important, and this includes letting them learn to deal with situations as they come up. He's tired of Chondra being so controlling about their weekend plans, so lately he's taken to "spontaneously" offering to take the kids on an outdoor adventure on a Saturday morning. That way, she doesn't have time to outfit everyone with head-to-toe rain gear and a week's supply of organic granola, and a part of him hopes that Chondra will decide she can't come along.

Chondra thinks Hugh takes unnecessary risks with their kids, which makes her very nervous. Chondra isn't against fun—of course not!—but she knows that she watches the kids more carefully than Hugh does, and one thing is for sure: They rarely get hurt when she's with them. She believes that Hugh is too cavalier about accidents; "It's a natural part of childhood," is his favorite response to her worries. She gets especially angry when he directly contradicts her, like the time she said the kids had to wear pants when hiking in a tick-filled forest. He argued with her in front of them, saying they could wear shorts since it was summer. She's tired of being cast as the crazy one for just trying to protect her kids. To her, it's Hugh who has gone off the deep end with his over-the-top plans. She's beginning to feel she can't trust him to be alone with the kids.

> He would think nothing of taking them skydiving if I don't put my foot down. He doesn't watch them closely enough even when they are just at the park.

> On his watch, Josie fell off a swing and had to get 8 stitches on her forehead!

> Sure, you can get a pocket knife

Hugh and Chondra's difference in how they approach parenting creates major conflict between them. Hugh bitterly criticizes Chondra for being overprotective and Chondra furiously attacks Hugh for being irresponsible. They both feel stuck and can't imagine how they could ever solve this dilemma. They both say, "My partner's personality is the problem!"

The Parenting Differences Fight does seem unsolvable at first. After all, how can anyone expect someone's personality to change enough to agree on such an essential issue as how to raise kids? Will Chondra suddenly become less risk-averse or will Hugh suddenly become more safety-conscious? Not likely.

But then again, how did such polar opposites ever end up together as a couple?

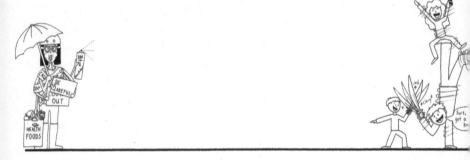

As we see Chondra and Hugh today, they seem so different from one another and so mismatched. Why did they ever want to be together if they're so completely different? Surely, even before they had kids, they must have had trouble with this dramatic difference between them!

But they weren't always this way. At the beginning of their relationship, and when they first became parents, things looked quite different.

At the beginning, Chondra wasn't the only one conscious of their child's safety, and Hugh wasn't the only one dreaming about family adventures. Even though they seem so different now, they actually started out *sharing* the values that underlie the fight. But over time, things began to shift.

With each new parenting experience, as Chondra sees Hugh being less cautious than she'd like, she starts to feel more fear for the children and moves toward more protective reactions. Hugh sees Chondra's overly worried behavior and feels aggravated that it limits his and the children's freedom, so he pushes to do even more exciting things with them.

When Chondra notices Hugh planning all these out-of-the-box "broadening experiences," she feels compelled to help him set some reasonable limits. Those limits drive Hugh to feel increasingly confined—he can't do what he wants to as a father. Chondra and Hugh start to come to some stark conclusions about one another:

Over time, Chondra becomes the flag-bearer for caution in the relationship, and Hugh starts to seem less and less careful. Similarly, Hugh starts to become the flag-bearer for fun experiences with the kids, and Chondra seems to always pass up the fun. As these differences grow more exaggerated, Chondra's and Hugh's roles become fixed in place. Hugh does focus a lot on planning activities without limits because no one else is doing it, and he wants the kids to have a life full of exciting experiences. And, on some level, he knows he doesn't have to keep close track of safety; Chondra will take care of that. Likewise, Chondra doesn't have to expend energy dreaming up adventures for the family because Hugh covers that job fine without her. The fight becomes polarized.

It's important to note that couples don't consciously *decide* to become flag-bearers for certain values. Polarization is often a gradual, unconscious drift that occurs in response to what you perceive as increasingly extreme behavior from your partner.

Polarized fights have certain patterns:

One Value Each – In a polarized fight, each partner argues for only one of two important values and appears not to care as much about the second value.

In Hugh and Chondra's fight, the two key conflicting values that drive their argument are (1) the importance of safety, and (2) the importance of having enjoyable experiences. At this point, it appears that only Chondra cares about the kids' safety and that only Hugh cares about the kids having fun.

One-Sided Reasoning – In a polarized fight, each partner explains their reasoning with a focus only on their respective value.

Suppose Chondra and Hugh are planning for a vacation with the kids during an upcoming school break. Hugh suggests going camping and Chondra agrees. They end up arguing for a while as they pack since Chondra wants to bring a lot of supplies that Hugh feels are unnecessary, but finally they get on the road. They set up their tent and start looking at the trail map. Hugh suggests they do the hike the park is famous for, the one that goes under the waterfall and through the dense forest. Chondra stops him there.

Notice that *all* of Chondra's reasoning revolves around safety, and *all* of Hugh's reasoning revolves around the fun experience the kids will have. Each partner's rationale relates only to his or her particular values. When the fight gets heated, they might even lecture one another on the importance of the value that speaks to them.

Outrage at Ignored Values – In a polarized fight, partners frequently react to the other's overemphasis on one value with outrage that the other value is being ignored.

Chondra can't believe that Hugh doesn't recognize the safety concerns of this hike. Hugh is amazed that Chondra could so blatantly ignore the kids' need to have fun. When they each hear how the other harps on only one value, it's infuriating! Hugh hears, "safety, safety, safety," and naturally asks, "How can you not consider fun?" Chondra hears, "fun, fun, fun," and naturally asks, "How can you not consider safety?"

Opposite Solutions – In a polarized fight, resolutions are difficult because the solutions each partner proposes are often exact opposites of one another:

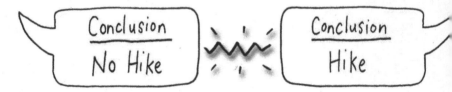

Chondra and Hugh can't go hiking and at the same time also *not* go hiking; it just isn't possible. They can keep arguing about whose solution to use, but neither is likely to give in. Both feel their reasoning is sound, and both Chondra and Hugh feel that their point of view is obviously right and therefore their solution is the one to go with. Neither is willing to concede to the other's solution because that would mean giving up on a value that's really important!

Selective Listening – Polarized fights grow increasingly polarized over time because both partners feel they can already predict what the other will say. They become more and more sure that they won't be swayed by the other's reasoning, sometimes without even hearing it: Why bother listening when they've heard the same logic a thousand times before? Clearly nothing has actually changed since the last time they had practically the same argument!

Since Chondra and Hugh have stopped listening to one another's reasoning, there's no chance they can reach a compromise; neither one will able to convince the other that their way is right.

In a nutshell, polarized fights look like this:

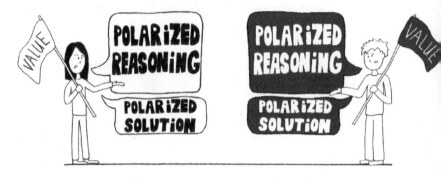

As an issue becomes more and more polarized, each partner becomes the flag-bearer for one of two important values. When a situation comes up that involves these values, they each present their polarized reasoning without listening to the other's reasoning and come up with two opposing solutions that have very little potential for compromise.

STOPPING THE PARENTING DIFFERENCES FIGHT

The key to stopping a polarized fight like the Parenting Differences Fight is to first recognize that, in reality, the underlying values aren't as polarized as they appear.

For example, if you asked Chondra if she wants her children to have fun and broadening experiences, she'd say that she definitely does, as long as those experiences aren't overly dangerous. If you asked Hugh if he cares about his children's safety, he'd say that he absolutely does and would never do anything to jeopardize their children's welfare. At the core, Chondra and Hugh both feel that safety and broadening experiences are important. But as the fight grew progressively more polarized, they lost track of their common ground.

Imagine if Chondra and Hugh could recognize that they actually share the two values and that neither has to be so extreme about either one. This would be a pivotal step in the right direction. They'd then have to grapple with how to solve for both values in situations that seem to pit safety and fun against one another. The only workable solutions would be those that incorporate both values.

This model for resolving the fight is not about "giving in" or compromising against your values. It's about reclaiming your interest in values that you may have lost sight of and working with your partner to take one another's concerns into account.

Here's how Chondra and Hugh resolve their fight about the hike on their camping trip: First they recognize together that the fight represents polarized values.

Chondra and Hugh identify that the two values underlying their constant arguments are safety and fun. They then acknowledge the importance of both of these values in making a decision about whether to go on the hike or not. They need to speak with equal concern about both values, taking extra care to pay attention to the value for which they were previously *not* the flag-bearer. Doing so reassures the other that, while they may not have articulated it previously, they too care about that value, so the one partner no longer feels compelled to push the other to care about it.

BOTH HOLD BOTH VALUES
(especially the ones they previously ignored)

A hike would be fun. Let's figure out which one to do...

What a relief! I don't have to convince her to have fun.

But let's make sure it's a hike that's also safe.

What a relief! I don't have to remind him about safety.

The conversation continues with both partners presenting reasoning that reflects both values:

I'm worried about it being a little cold today for a hike, but we have been in the car all morning and it would be great to get the kids out and moving.

The hike under the waterfall looks like so much fun, but it might be a little long to do just in an afternoon.

That hike is also in a pretty dense vegetation area ...

True, we'd have to change into long pants if we did that one.

Look, here's one that has a hanging bridge over a stream — that could be fun!

And that one we could probably finish easily this afternoon, so we wouldn't have to worry about getting back to the campsite when it's really cold.

If we wake up early tomorrow we might also have time to do the waterfall hike before we head home.

If the weather holds up...

Because Hugh and Chondra keep both values in mind as they sort out what hike to go on, they can flexibly present reasons that consider both safety concerns and a desire to have fun. The conversation doesn't descend into polarization and insulting characterizations of one another. Instead, they stay focused on the challenge of finding a hike that's both fun and safe.

You might be thinking, what if there were no alternate hike they could do and they had to decide either to do the waterfall hike or not? The key to stopping this fight is not about finding a handy compromise that makes everyone happy; it's about both partners recognizing that neither can be happy unless the underlying values are jointly held and both partners' concerns are addressed.

Here are two possible solutions to the hike dilemma that do not include a convenient alternate hike:

1. They decide to go on the more adventurous waterfall hike, taking as many safety precautions as they can, and Hugh stays sensitive to, and understanding of, Chondra's fears about safety. In fact, he makes sure that he's the voice of safety alerts as they hike.

2. They decide not to go on the waterfall hike, and Chondra stays sensitive to Hugh's disappointment about not going. She recognizes that it's a loss for him and finds a way to be the initiator of other fun activities during the camping trip.

In the first example, Hugh holds both values for the couple—he's in charge of balancing both safety and fun. In the second, Chondra holds both values and makes sure that if fun is sacrificed in one instance, it needs to be emphasized later. In both examples, they're each freed from being one-value flag-bearers that are at odds with one another, allowing them to stop the fight.

THE PARENTING DIFFERENCES FIGHT TOOLBOX

When you find that you and your partner repeatedly have opposing ideas about parenting, consider that the fight has become polarized.

Identify the two values that are driving the conflicting sides.

Commit together to come back from the polarized positions.

Discuss solutions to parenting problems as you both hold *both* of the key values.

CHAPTER 10

THE MONEY FIGHT

IT'S SO COMMON IT'S ALMOST a cliché: Couples fight about money. So it's not surprising that there's *a lot* of advice out there how to stop fighting about finances.

While some couples might find this advice helpful, the battles about money usually aren't about a couple failing to set their saving and spending priorities together. The Money Fight generally happens because a couple *can't agree* about their financial priorities in the first place. To stop a Money Fight, let's consider *why* people act the way they do with money.

When it comes to money, our motivations are very basic. Money can represent dreams—dreams of freedom, potential for the future, comfort, and security. But because money is a limited resource, it can also ignite our fears.

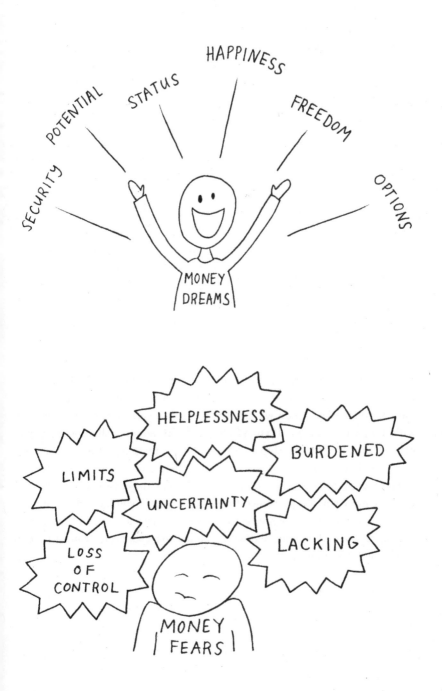

The threats of not having enough or losing what we do have can easily drive most of us into Defense Mode.

The instinctive human response to the threat of losing financial security is to be extra protective about money. It makes sense; if you feel insecure about money, you're likely to do whatever you can to regain control. Your history with money matters, too. If you've often felt that money is slipping away, you may be more likely to develop a Defense Mode defined by extra financial caution, to help ensure that it doesn't. On the other hand, if you feel someone is always limiting what you spend, it's natural to want to get away from that control. The more you feel prevented from enjoying what you have, the more you seek to find ways to enjoy it anyway. And if you have a history of frequently feeling deprived of happiness and joy, you may have an even stronger urge to relish that freedom to spend.

These common responses to threats of deprivation and loss of control set us up for arguments about money.

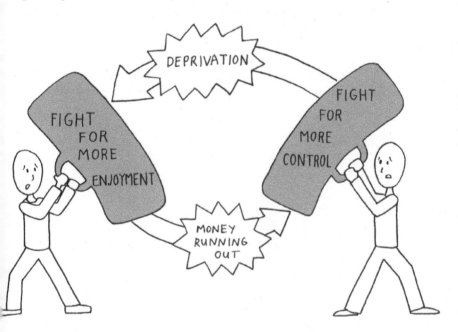

If you feel your partner is depriving you by being too controlling about money, you're likely to react by fighting for even more enjoyment. The fight for enjoyment often involves an increase in spending, which ignites your partner's fears that the money will run out. The threat of loss of security naturally leads to an attempt to get finances under control. Fighting for more control consequently triggers feelings of deprivation in the other partner, and an endless cycle ensues. While it's reasonable and natural to protect against threats we perceive, those defensive actions can inadvertently send out more threats, *amplifying* the fears we're trying to avoid rather than alleviating them. As a result, most conflicts about money involve some dynamic where one partner is characterized as the "spender" and the other as the "saver." But the way partners describe one another in money fights tend to be a bit more unflattering.

A POLARIZED FIGHT

When Molly and Samuel fight about money, here's what Molly says to Samuel:

Here's what Samuel says to Molly:

Molly and Samuel have a major disconnect about their lifestyle when it comes to money; they're on opposite ends of the spending spectrum.

As with the Parenting Differences Fight (see Chapter 9), the Money Fight often becomes more polarized as time goes on. Molly and Samuel may have started out with somewhat similar attitudes toward money, but over time, their reactions to one another's behavior move them farther and farther apart.

At the beginning of their relationship, both Molly and Samuel were conscious of enjoying what their money could buy while being careful not to overspend. But little by little, as Samuel sees that Molly spends more freely than he does, it starts to make him anxious. So he gets a bit thriftier to compensate and perhaps show her a different way to approach shopping. When Molly sees Samuel becoming more careful about money, she begins to feel restricted. She might try to assert herself more by being a bit looser about money and by encouraging him not to be so controlling.

If this fight grows even more polarized, Samuel might begin to withhold money even more and Molly might in turn get more cavalier about spending, and the fight would intensify. Anticipating one another's reactions, and fearful of starting yet another fight, they begin to hide what they do with money from one another.

It's almost as if Molly and Samuel are both saying to themselves, "If I can't get what I want in this Money Fight by working *with* my partner, I'll get what I want by working around them." Resolving the Money Fight when it's moved to hiding and secrets can be very difficult. Each partner feels worried about revealing what he or she hasn't previously told the other about their saving or spending because they know the reaction they'll get—anger and a return to the fight. Hiding their strategies can seem easier than dealing directly with one another about money.

Now imagine how impossible it would be for Molly and Samuel to follow the financial advice from the experts.

Opening a conversation about making a budget or setting financial priorities ignites the conflict every time. If avoiding the topic or not quite telling the whole truth has become the best way to head off having the fight, they are right to be worried about opening up a dialogue. How productive could it possibly be?

But there *is* a way out. If Molly and Samuel take a step back and recognize that their Money Fight is polarized, they can come back from that polarization and stop the fight.

First, let's compare the Money Fight to the characteristics of polarized fights described in the Parenting Differences Fight (see Chapter 9):

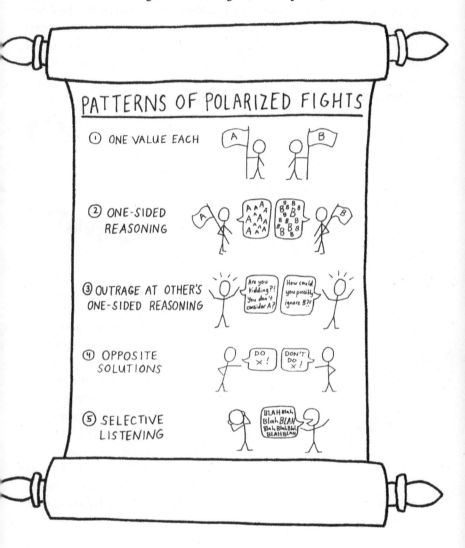

ONE VALUE EACH

What are the underlying values for which Molly and Samuel are the flag-bearers in their Money Fight? Both sides have legitimate core values at the heart of their approach to money. For the saver in a Money Fight, it's not about holding on to money just to have a pile of the stuff. Saving money provides *security*, a sense of safety and reliability.

When he's built up a nest egg, Samuel feels calm knowing that if either he or Molly were to lose their job, they could survive without suffering. Just having the money in the bank gives him a strong foundation of comfort and lets him deal more confidently with the other stresses of every-day life. He doesn't mind passing up expensive clothes or a new car because the feeling of secu-rity is more valuable to him.

For the spender in a Money Fight, money is about more than having access to the finer things in life. Spending money gives a fantastic feeling of *freedom*—the ability to choose something you like, to live a life unlimited by financial practi-cality.

When Molly buys the phone she really wants—not giving up extra features just to save money—she feels genuine joy. She enjoys that positive feeling every time she uses her phone, which makes dealing with the other stresses of life more manage-able. She'd rather add pressure on herself to make more money next month than give up that intoxicating feeling of freedom and satisfaction.

ONE-SIDED REASONING, OPPOSING SOLUTIONS, AND OUTRAGE AT IGNORED VALUES

When Molly argues with Samuel about money, her reasoning is that having money is about feeling joy through freedom: "You have to splurge once in awhile!" or "What's the point in depriving yourself?" Samuel argues right back that having money is about feeling joy through security: "We'll feel so much better if we have a nest egg!" or "We won't have to worry about getting the rent paid."

From an objective standpoint, both arguments are compelling and reasonable. But Samuel and Molly see only their own side of the argument as reasonable and believe their partner's point of view is just wrong. Molly feels outraged that Samuel doesn't want to enjoy life, while Samuel can't believe that Molly isn't concerned about their financial security. They continue to lecture one another and ignore one another's reasoning because they've heard it a hundred times before. They press for opposing solutions that don't work for the other party.

Molly's solution doesn't work for Samuel because it doesn't solve his concerns about security. She attempts to get him to give her more freedom by offering him freedom to spend as well, which isn't what the Money Fight is about for him. Having them both spending lots of money makes the problem bigger for him, not smaller.

Samuel might also come up with a one-sided solution:

I'll give her an allowance – that way she can spend it but it won't be too much.

How about I give you x dollars a month to spend however you'd like?

Oh, so now you are giving me an allowance?!? What am I a child?

Samuel's solution doesn't work for Molly because it feels like just another way for him to control her. Under his "allowance" plan, Molly doesn't feel the freedom and trust that she craves—she senses that he views her as childish and in need of a "parent" to set her straight. Samuel's solution is one-sided because the main goal *is* to control Molly's spending.

Interestingly, if Samuel had offered his solution while demonstrating that he also understood Molly's need for freedom, this same plan might have had greater success.

What's different about this approach? Samuel shows that he understands Molly's desire for occasional splurges and that he's not judging her for it. He also helps her see why that behavior is challenging for him, but he's able to do so in a way that doesn't place blame on her. He presents his solution in a manner that addresses their mutual problem as "our tendency to fight about money," rather than Molly's "spending problem."

STOPPING THE MONEY FIGHT

Here are some ways of approaching the Money Fight that can help you come to a real solution, not just a short-term bandage. Each one of the following tools can be used for a variety of polarized fights, not just those about money.

AGREE ON THE RIGHT PROBLEM

As we saw in Samuel's second approach, a key way to break free from a Money Fight is to first take a look at the conflict as a whole. Agree that the fight is a problem for both of you, that you both contribute to it, and that you both want to it to change.

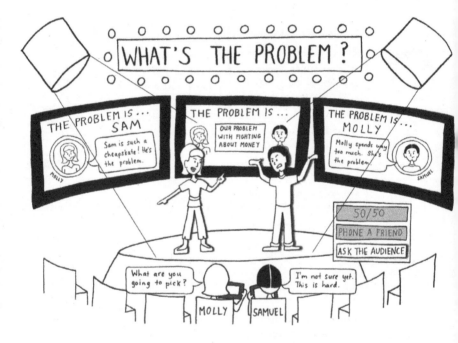

With a Big Picture View of their fight, Samuel and Molly can identify and agree on the real problem they need to solve. If they insist that the other person is the problem, the solutions they propose will keep the fight going: Samuel tries to solve the Molly-the-Spender problem by being defensively controlling, and Molly tries to solve the Samuel-the-Tightwad problem by defensively spending. Neither of them wants to sign up to solve an issue that essentially names him- or herself as the problem! The We-Fight-Too-Much-About-Money problem is one that can be agreed upon by both parties and jointly solved. Naming the problem as a mutually created one, in which neither partner is blamed, gets both partners more engaged in solving it.

COME BACK FROM POLARIZATION

The Money Fight often polarizes into a fight between security and freedom, where it seems as if each partner only cares about one of the involved values. Imagine if Samuel could tell Molly that he really does understand her wish for freedom, that it's a legitimate desire, and that he wants freedom, too, in addition to security. Imagine if Molly could empathize with Samuel's fears about financial security rather than accusing him of being a tightwad. Once they understand that both values are important to each of them and that they've just become polarized over time, they have an opportunity to reclaim both values. Now when solving money issues, Molly and Samuel work together to find a solution that preserves both partners' security and freedom.

THINK BEYOND SIMPLE COMPROMISE

Money decisions can sometimes appear to be a matter of simple compromise: "OK, we will save half and spend half." But splitting the difference doesn't always satisfy the key values involved.

For example, when Molly's bonus check comes in, Samuel argues that they should use it to pay down their student loans to lighten their debt load, so that they'll more easily qualify for a mortgage when they need it. Molly wants to use the bonus for a nice vacation because they've both worked very hard all year and deserve a break. They argue about it for a while and both feel frustrated with the other's priorities, but they eventually agree to use some for the loans and some for the vacation. This compromise may stop the fight temporarily because it seems roughly *fair*, but both might still feel resentment. For Samuel, paying off only a little bit of debt doesn't deplete the loan enough to really make him feel any more secure. And Molly thinks, "With only half the money to spend on vacation, it probably isn't going to be such a great vacation."

Neither one of them is actually happy about the divide-the-bonus solution. Both Samuel and Molly still feel alone in their objective for a nice vacation or the relief of lessening their debt. The simple compromise doesn't work to solve what they care about most. If, on the other hand, they each worked to embrace both values, they would be able to talk about all the factors that affect their decision in an evenhanded manner. Their empathy for one another's dreams and fears about money would factor into the discussion and help them find a collaborative solution that truly satisfies both of them.

BOTH HOLD BOTH VALUES
(especially the ones they previously ignored)

We really should take a nice vacation. It would be good for us. It would also be great if we paid off our debts – that would feel like we're really moving forward. Hmm... how should we balance that we really want both?

Once both values are acknowledged and each partner stops advocating for only one value, opportunities arise for generosity and joint solutions. Molly might be willing to forgo the vacation this year if she knows that Samuel is just as interested as she is to go all-out next year. Samuel might be willing to handle the anxiety of another year of debt if he knows that the jointly planned vacation will be fun and that Molly actually cares just as much as he does about paying down the debt next year. It's not just what solution you agree to; it's what the spirit of that solution offers you as partners; if you both care about one another's wishes and fears, you can stop the fight.

UNDERSTAND THE IMPACT OF EMOTIONAL HISTORY AND EMPATHIZE WITH YOUR PARTNER

Many fights, including those about money, get especially intense because they carry the weight of history in them. Whether we realize it or not, every one of us has a life history with money that started in childhood. As children, we all experience the financial environment in our families, including how our parents managed money and how money was talked about.

Children have strong feelings, both conscious and subconscious, about what they observe and hear, and they take away lessons that can deeply affect how they feel about money as adults. Let's consider some childhood stories about money.

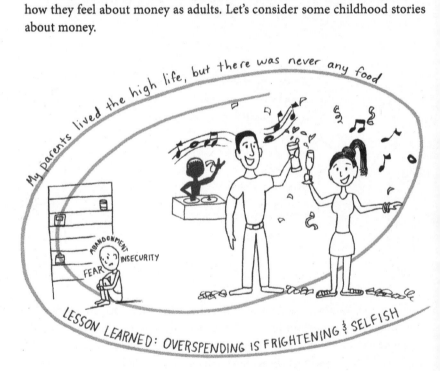

My family was the fun one, and my uncle was the tightwad.

I bet Uncle John's family is having a great time counting their money at home!

SUPERIOR
HAPPY
PROUD

LESSON LEARNED: SAVERS MISS OUT

My father knew what poverty was and never wanted us to forget...

When I was a boy, my family lost everything...

RELIEVED
CAUTIOUS
SECURE

LESSON LEARNED: DON'T WASTE YOUR GOOD FORTUNE

These are just a few simplified examples of the very strong feelings and opinions we form during childhood about the "way to deal with money." Our experiences are complex and full of many possible interpretations of events. No one can predict what lesson any individual will learn from their particular family history about money (siblings often take away very different lessons), nor can one predict which financial events will be the ones that make a lasting impression. However, whatever we do learn in childhood gets carried consciously or unconsciously into our romantic relationships.

Sometimes we believe that what our parents did was about right and we try to emulate it; other times we promise ourselves we'll do something very, very differently. Either way, the feelings we experienced aren't forgotten. If you felt fear, insecurity, and abandonment as a result of your parents' spending money that should have been for food, that threat can easily be triggered when your partner suddenly comes home with an expensive and unnecessary new gadget. It's almost as if there's a memory chip locked in your brain that carries your old fears, dreams, stories, and pains about money. When your partner does something that activates those feelings, your reaction may be a lot bigger than the situation warrants because the weight of history amplifies it.

When Jasmine offers her opinion about buying the barbeque, Kane feels the familiar threat of someone controlling spending and he instinctively reacts to it by angrily shaking off her control. While he isn't thinking about it at the time, it's the kind of response he wishes his mother had said to his controlling father—"Get off my back; you're being unfair!" Jasmine is surprised by his strong reaction—it doesn't seem reasonable to her; she was simply offering her opinion.

If Kane tells her she's being controlling, she might feel angry at being accused in such a way and she might get defensive, too. A whole fight will launch, seemingly about whether they can buy the barbeque. Really, though, this fight isn't about the barbeque. It's about the old memory chip that Kane still carries with him that makes him extra sensitive to being told "no" about money. Of course, since every one of us comes with our own built-in memory chips, it gets even more complex when both partners' histories are triggered:

Although it might seem like this couples' frustration is just about the current situation, in fact it's the individual money histories encoded in each of their memories that are driving this fight. In their conversation, Chloe expects some appreciation from her husband, Tim, that she got so much for so little money—similar to the pride she felt in her mother for scrimping and saving. She immediately feels annoyed that he isn't giving her credit for her big win. Tim, on the other hand, sees Chloe's clearance buying through the lens of his desire to be a good provider. Perhaps unconsciously, he wants his wife and children to feel as confident and proud in his ability to give them a comfortable life as he felt with his parents. Neither partner can see the memory chip operating in the other's head, so it isn't obvious why buying clearance means such different things to each one. As this fight unfolds, they try to explain to the other why they should or shouldn't buy on clearance, but they're not getting to the heart of the matter, which is that each of their histories makes clearance either a source of great pride or a sign of insult.

Well, you may be asking, if you can't change history, how can you stop this fight?

Here's a good first step: Outside of the heat of the moment of fighting, take the time to understand both your own history and your partner's history and use that to examine why you each have especially strong reactions to the situation you fight about. For example, it might take some introspection and consideration of his background for Tim to understand *why* buying clearance items feels so insulting. Once Chloe understands that his strong reaction is really about his desire to be seen as a great provider for the family, she can feel compassion toward his point of view. It suddenly makes sense to her; she understands that his anger about clearance shopping actually comes from a very positive intention. And Tim can begin to understand that Chloe's position in the fight is a result of her desire to feel pride in doing her part for the family's finances. With empathy for one another's intentions, new options for solving this fight emerge.

Sometimes, couples can't reach this level of dialogue because each partner insists that the only way to view the situation is through his or her own lens: "*Anyone* would be insulted if they made enough money and their wife brought home clearance!" or "Getting a bargain is *clearly* something to be proud of—how can you be upset about it?!" Although our personal view often seems to be the only "obvious" way to think about a situation, as we can see from this example, both views are actually legitimate—and which way you go depends a lot on your history. Couples who come to their relationship with different life histories, as most do, will find that they have very different perspectives that can easily ignite fights.

Here's a couple who had a bitter fight earlier about whether they should invest in a fund one of their friends recommended. Several of their other friends had invested, but Dennis insisted that it was too risky. Clark was furious that Dennis wouldn't even consider it. Dennis argued that Clark was being irresponsible. After the fight, they discussed what went wrong.

For Clark, the feeling of putting his hard-earned future at risk is enough of a deterrent to skip the investment, something he happened to learn from his father. For Dennis, feeling left out of something exciting because of an unwillingness to spend money triggers the family story of dumb Uncle John who always missed out because he was too guarded with his money.

Notice that Dennis and Clark don't have to psychoanalyze one another to be able to resolve this fight. They describe what their core feelings are about the issue, and they listen to the other's feelings and accept that those feelings are reasonable and important to pay attention to. Clark doesn't criticize Dennis's wish not to be left out; he accepts it as important to Dennis and a legitimate concern. Dennis doesn't mock Clark's very conservative approach; instead, he hears it as a real source of anxiety for Clark and therefore important to consider. While they don't talk directly about the history that drives their feelings, they understand the shadow it casts. Clark knows how Dennis came to be a person who is sensitive to feeling left out, and Dennis knows that Clark has good reason to be risk-averse. They don't try to change one another; they accept that this is how the other is. In the end, their solution takes each partner's needs into account. In this case, a half-and-half compromise works because the solution actually meets both key values—Clark's need to be cautious, and Dennis's need not to miss out on opportunity.

So how much do you understand about the reasons why your partner is the way he or she is? What are the important stories and experiences in his or her life history that influence your partner's feelings and approach to life now? It's equally important to understand your own history and what formed your personal values. That introspection will help you repair many kinds of fights, not just the Money Fight. It provides you with the ability to talk about why your reactions are strong, and it helps both you and your partner separate your current reactions from the feelings from the past.

Every one of us has sensitivities and vulnerabilities from past experiences, which we carry around in our core. For example, if you had a girlfriend cheat on you in the past, you're probably more worried than you were before that it might happen again, and your future relationships will be impacted by that reduced sense of trust that you feel. But, as we saw earlier, the most impactful experiences—the ones that tend to really stick with us and form our strongest opinions—are the ones from childhood.

Our childhood experiences shape our worldview so very deeply because, as children, we are most vulnerable and impressionable. We learn what the world is like, what people are like, and what we can expect from our relationships with others from exposure to the first relationships of our lives. However, even though those first relationships with parents or caregivers or siblings help shape how we think and feel, it would be wrong to say that we can blame all our problems today on those early experiences alone. It would also be problematic to excuse current bad behavior by saying, "I can't help it; I had a bad childhood." So what's the productive way to use your past history to stop fights and have better communication with your partner?

USING YOUR HISTORY TO SOLVE THE MONEY FIGHT (AND OTHER FIGHTS)

Each person's emotional history builds the core of who he or she is. When we fall in love, we fall in love with the core of our partner. Often, partners tell one another stories about their emotional history when they first get together. They share the dreams and pains of their life story, and their partners react with love, empathy, and support: "Wow, you survived such hardship and look how great you are!" or "Your relatives are tough and yet you're so different from your family!" or "Your life built you into the amazing person that you are." Whether life was difficult or easy, in the throes of love, your lover sees you as the hero of your life, the best one in your family, and you see your partner as the hero of his or her life story, too.

But as time goes on, the "hero" view fades and we can start to see our partner as the *flawed victim* of their life story. Our love, empathy, and support turn to criticism: "You're *just like* your snobby family!" or "No wonder you act the way you do—your parents were *crazy!*" or "Of course you can't express caring—*you grew up like a robot!*" When fights with a history component erupt, we're more likely to call our partner's behavior "pathological" than to find a way to use history to empathize.

You *can* use history to stop the Money Fight, or any other fight, if you use it to empathize, not pathologize. Consider your partner's life story. Can you see how he or she came to have the vulnerabilities, fears, dreams, and pain that he or she has? If so, your understanding of your partner's history can lead to compassion. Imagine how hard it was for your partner to live that story. What fortitude did it take to survive and thrive? How would any person feel if they grew up in that environment?

Interestingly, compassion is also important even if your partner's past history wasn't too difficult. It can be genuinely challenging for a person who hasn't experienced family struggles around money to "get" how powerful those struggles feel for a partner; it isn't obvious to them why certain dynamics around money feel so painful. When they react without understanding, the temptation is for their partner to respond with anger and accusations of insensitivity. Compassion works here, too.

Having empathy for your partner's history is the key tool to be able to break free from fights that are driven by the engine of history.

With this new empathetic mindset toward your partner, you can stop the Money Fight by talking about what you understand about your partner's core: "I realize that it's hard for you to have restrictions on spending because naturally it brings up old feelings of deprivation. I don't want to do that to you!" And in the other direction: "I know that it's hard for you to live with fear of financial insecurity, especially given your past. Of course you're worried about that—and I don't want you to feel that fear again. How can we work together to keep that from happening?"

To summarize, Money Fights are tough because major dreams and fears are at stake. The fights can easily become polarized and then intensified by the shadows of past history. Stopping the Money Fight is about finding ways to take into account both values of security *and* freedom. Solutions need to reduce the fear of ruin *and* the fear of deprivation. Focusing on the underlying values of a Money Fight allows you to go beyond simple compromises and find real solutions that everyone can live with. And, most important, when both partners cultivate compassion and empathy for one another's sensitivities about money, they can truly stop the Money Fight for good.

POSTSCRIPT

A final word about the Money Fight: While there are many kinds of fights about money, in this chapter I chose to focus on one significant kind of Money Fight—the spender/saver kind. Couples fight about more than just spending and saving, of course. They fight about whether a partner is working hard enough to provide for the family, or whether it's OK to lend money to family members, or how to teach their children about money. They fight about debts and inheritances, about how much each partner should work, and about the proper way to keep track of finances. All of these fights have elements of the spender/saver fight. In each one, we argue from the core for security and freedom and we fight through the triggers of history.

A few words, too, about history: A person's story doesn't necessarily have to be dramatic or traumatic to have an impact on how a person approaches fights about money. It could be that you grew up in a family of savers, where everyone was careful with money and where you heard lessons about being cautious, so saving has become your natural habit. Your partner may have had an equally non-traumatic childhood, but their family members were generally freer with money, establishing a habit of comfort with spending. Such a couple would still have to navigate their way through their differences. A mutual understanding of how habits are formed by childhood experiences will help make discussions about money less judgmental and less likely to evolve into fights.

THE MONEY FIGHT TOOLBOX

 Agree on the right problem—the joint one rather than the blaming ones.

 Come back from polarization.

 Think beyond simple compromise.

 Understand the impact of emotional history and empathize with your partner.

CHAPTER 11

THE SEX FIGHT

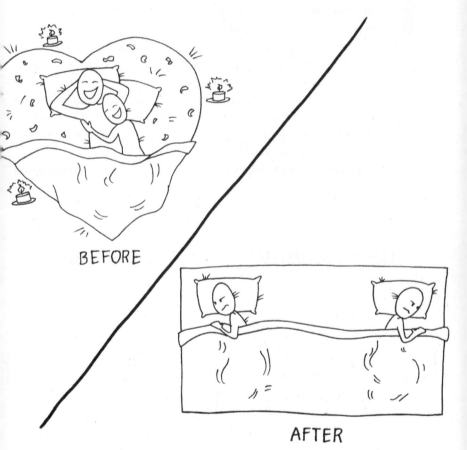

BEFORE

AFTER

IT'S ALWAYS ON THE "Top Ten Things Couples Fight About" lists. We love sex, but sometimes it creates a lot of conflict. Unfortunately, there are plenty of problems that can cause trouble in a couple's sex life, but the Sex Fight is the anger, arguing, and acrimony *about* sex. Something feels awry in your sexual connection, so you open up a conversation about it with your partner, and *bam*—there's a fight. The fight doesn't bring you any closer to getting what you need sexually, and it just makes things worse. If only you could stop this repetitive fight before it happens, maybe *then* there could be a productive conversation about improving your sex life.

The Sex Fight starts with dissatisfaction. And there's *a lot* of dissatisfaction out there:

"IT'S NOT ROMANTIC"

"IT'S TOO BORING"

"HE NEVER WANTS IT ANYMORE"

"IT'S NOT ENOUGH"

"IT'S TOO SHORT"

"WE NEVER HAVE THE SEX I WANT"

"HE DOESN'T DO WHAT I LIKE"

"SHE'S ALWAYS TOO TIRED"

Ideally, sex is exciting, plentiful, responsive, varied, and there when we need it. When reality doesn't measure up, it's extremely frustrating, and dissatisfaction leads to fights about sex. Interestingly, sexual performance is an area of human experience that seems to attract an unusual amount of evaluation. "How was that for you?"—the classic after-sex question—goes right to the heart of it. It's irresistible to wonder: Did you like it as much as I did? Did you like *what* I did? Was it amazing? Was it good enough? Sometimes the evaluations get out of hand and the assumptions, expectations, and interpretations that arise can create tension.

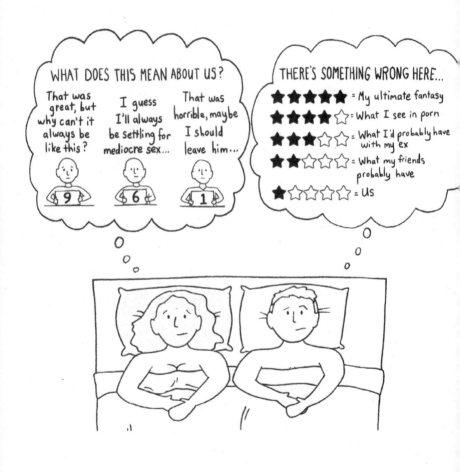

Constantly measuring your sex life against assumptions of what it should be like, or what others must be getting, or what you had with a different partner can get dangerous. It highlights dissatisfaction and prompts judgment about your partner. Mix that judgment with the human tendency toward insecurity about sexual performance, and you can see how the evaluation of your sex life can be a major factor in kicking off the Sex Fight.

Imagine how it would sound if we applied the same degree of evaluation to other aspects of life:

Most of us don't assess our own and our partner's biological needs and draw worried conclusions about the state of our relationships: "Oh no, you got more out of your night's rest than I did—how selfish of you . . . !"

Consider what would happen if we brought sex back into the realm of other biological pleasures: In the same way that some meals are more enjoyable than others, some sexual encounters will be better than others. We know that fretting over a mediocre meal doesn't make the next one better. And with sex, fretting, analyzing, and evaluating can actually make the next sexual encounter worse. We all greatly appreciate the joy of an especially delicious meal, but most of us don't have an expectation that *all* meals will be equally satisfying. Dropping that expectation about sex would help a lot.

And, hey, sex is play, not work. Play is all about having fun, messing around, and doing whatever you feel like in the moment without specific goals in mind. Play doesn't respond well to pressure, over-direction, or evaluation. Evaluating how well you play just turns it into work. If we could keep sex in the realm of play without applying judgments, expectations, and implications, more Sex Fights could be prevented.

Here's why: When you evaluate the sex you're having and feel disappointed by it, you're likely to take this approach:

Yes, getting your partner to change. It seems like the only way out: To get what you want out of sex, you've got to make your partner give it to you how you want it. So of course you try. And the most commonly offered advice out there backs you up: "Tell your partner what you like so that he or she can know how to please you."

Sometimes this can be quite helpful, since couples can learn a lot when they directly hear what would feel more pleasurable to their partners. But there's an unfortunate catch to this advice: Telling your partner how to change can accidentally launch a Partner Improvement Fight (see Chapter 1). Informing your partner that you would prefer something different can come across with a subtext that up until now, your partner has been getting it wrong.

Partner Improvement attempts are especially tricky when it comes to sex because many people harbor worries about their sexual competence: "Will I turn her on?" "Will he think I'm sexy?" Sure, you can walk around believing you're wonderful in bed and not worry about what other people think, but since sex is a partner activity, the feedback you receive can puncture that confidence. One partner seemed to think you were pretty good, but another seemed unsatisfied, and now your current partner has a complaint. Is it you? Maybe it's them. How can you know? Even the most confident lovers can't help but notice feedback—why didn't she sound more excited during sex? Why did his hand linger on my belly . . . does he find it unattractive? Did she like it? Does he like me? Was that good for him? Was that good for her?

Because of that natural sensitivity, innocent suggestions to your partner about how to improve sex can sometimes come across as strong negative judgments.

"You're a **TERRIBLE** lover."

"There is something **WRONG** with you sexually."

"You've **FAILED**."

"You **DON'T KNOW** how to please someone."

"You are **NEVER** going to get any better at it!"

"You turn me **OFF**."

Feeling judged by your partner about your sexual ability feels like a big threat, and as we have seen starting from Chapter 6 (the Birthday Fight), threats will trigger Defense Mode. When you're feeling insecure or criticized about your sexual performance, Defense Mode often manifests as the urge to duck away and hide, distance from your partner, or maybe even engage *less* in sex.

Or, you do the most common thing; you blame your partner. This, unsurprisingly, touches off a Sex Fight.

Sometimes, of course, couples *can* find ways to gently make suggestions to their partners about sex without triggering one another's defenses. If requests are made with sensitivity and without judgment, you and your partner can work through disappointments about your sex life. But if what you say comes with a subtext of your partner being "wrong," Defense Mode can be triggered and the mutual blaming and downward spiral of the Sex Fight begins.

Over time, with both partners on guard and pointing fingers at one another, *any* suggestion to the other about how to be a better lover just fuels the fire with more feelings of judgment and blame. Both partners become defensive as their actions and words create more threats, driving one another deeper and deeper into Defense Mode. The fight continues—and the sex certainly doesn't get any better.

How can you get out of this minefield once it's begun? Let's look at an example of one of the most universal Sex Fights: the fight about frequency. Of course, there are many other types of arguments about sex, but this one is so common that many people assume it's unsolvable. Kate and Sid have been embroiled in this one for months. Here's how the problem looks from Sid's side:

In Sid's view of the situation, he's being rejected, deprived, or simply appeased—and none of those feel good. Worried, threatened thoughts might creep into his mind: Is she rejecting me because I turn her off? Or because I'm not a good lover? Does she give in because she pities me? But then come the more self-comforting, defensive thoughts: "Nah—I haven't changed. Something must be wrong with her."

Kate's side of the story looks like this:

Kate feels justified in putting distance between herself and Sid because she believes he's being unreasonable. But she also feels the creep of worried, threatened thoughts. "What *is* wrong with me? What happened to my desire? I used to be able to switch into sex quickly but now I just can't. Maybe it *is* my fault . . . maybe I'm just not really a sexual person."

She begins to believe that the difference in desire is her fault because it's her body that seems not able to cooperate. So sometimes she blames herself, but sometimes she goes to the more comfortable, defensive position of blaming Sid. Either way, it doesn't help her feel any more desire for him. Soon, from that simple difference in desire, a predictable pattern of dynamics emerges as both parties try to solve the respective challenges they face.

Sid puzzles over how to get Kate to have sex with him when she never seems to want it. Here's what Sid or others in his position often do:

He tries it all: flattery, coming up with romantic activities, repeated attempts to initiate sex, complaining, and turning over responsibility. Kate may be frustrated with Sid's efforts, but what he's doing makes a great deal of logical sense. He has no idea *when* Kate will finally agree to have sex with him, so why not keep trying, because hey, one of these days she might be in the mood.

He continues to work hard to get Kate into bed with him, but when nothing seems to work, he begins to believe that there must be something wrong with her and starts to lose hope that she'll ever change. Quite understandably, he decides to give up trying to initiate sex, and then he stews about it. He makes a plan to just wait to see if she'll make the first move. That lasts a bit, until she doesn't make any moves, and he imagines a sexless future. Feeling panicked that it's up to him to prevent total deprivation, he eventually tries again, expecting nothing new from her. He feels that at least he's *attempting* to do something about it, while Kate seems to do nothing to help solve the problem. He feels both desperate and hopeless at the same time.

On Kate's side, she wants to figure out how to change the dynamic from being about sex under pressure to being about sex that reignites her desire. Here's what Kate and others in her position often try:

Kate's actions make sense as she tries to deal with her dissatisfaction. Sid's requests for sex have started to seem too frequent, and the sex seems too disconnected from love or romance. Kate isn't sure why she isn't feeling as much desire these days, but she theorizes that her loss of desire might be because of Sid's recent approach to sex. Maybe if Sid seduced her with romance as he used to, she'd feel more in the mood. So she asks him for more romance before sex, or she avoids having sex when she isn't really in the mood, so that when they do have it, the experience will be more satisfying in the way she hopes.

But then, when she sees Sid so obviously doing something romantic just as a prelude to sex, she grows annoyed because that makes her feel like he's trying to control her—put a romantic dinner in, get sex out. So she might avoid the back rub because it feels manipulative to her. At other times, even when she isn't completely in the mood, she agrees to have sex because she feels bad about saying no so often and figures, "why not?" But during those times, Kate isn't very enthusiastic. All these various efforts to deal with her side of the problem send mixed messages to Sid and don't really solve anything anyway. She feels unsatisfied about this state of affairs but also feels unable to change it.

So here they are: Sid and Kate are both working to shift the pattern in their relationship by trying to encourage the other person to change, but their actions drive a vicious cycle.

Sid's actions—hinting, asking, waiting, and complaining—come across as pressure on Kate. They make her feel judged if she doesn't, or used if she does. All Kate's actions—avoiding or giving in halfheartedly—come across to Sid as rejection, and they make him feel deprived and unable to get what he wants. The more rejected Sid feels, the more he tries to change the situation by doing more asking, hinting, waiting, and complaining. The more pressure Kate feels, the more she tries to alleviate it by avoiding Sid or giving him a lukewarm reception. The threats they each feel drive Defense Mode, which, in turn, drives the cycle.

So how can Sid and Kate break this cycle and stop the Sex Fight? It's helpful to first understand what triggers the whole thing: Kate and Sid are currently mismatched in their sexual desire. His is higher; hers is lower. He wants more; she's fine with less. Those are the facts for now. But then come the inevitable assumptions and explanations of those facts:

* "Her wanting less *means* I don't turn her on."
* "My lower desire *means* there's something wrong with me."
* "Our mismatched libidos *means* I picked the wrong partner."
* "Her not wanting sex as much *means* she doesn't love me as much."
* "Not being good in bed anymore for him *means* he'll leave me."
* "Turning me down again? I wonder if that *means* she's having an affair."

When we sense a mismatch in what's happening sexually, we almost always interpret it as something being wrong. It's as if we expect everything about sex to be aligned and when it isn't—uh-oh! Somehow the message we learn is that sex is supposed to smoothly flow like this:

Both partners are on the same ride. Their interest is the same, their timing is matched, and they both want to do this ride again, the same number of times. And sometimes it is like that . . . but often the reality is much more like this:

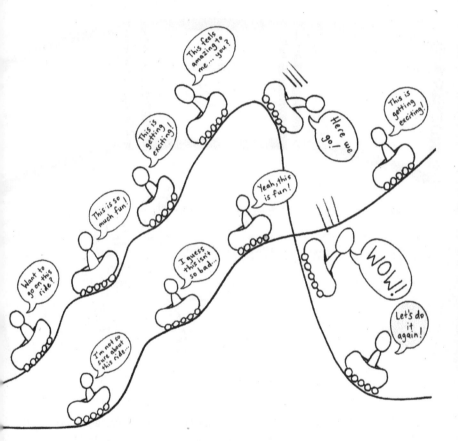

Often couples aren't on the same ride when it comes to sex, and it's not just the timing that's misaligned. Considering all the factors that can interfere, an "all systems go" alignment is actually pretty miraculous.

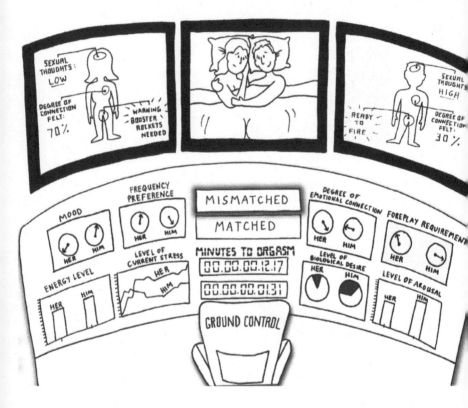

When it comes to sex, mismatches in timing, interest, desire, and mood are the *norm*, not the exception. If you consider how rare it is to be totally in sync with a partner, it's surprising that we believe these mismatches imply there's a problem. And yet we do. Anything other than a perfect matchup causes us to worry that something is wrong—wrong with me, wrong with you, or wrong with our relationship. Concern, judgment, and interpretation follow, which can cause more trouble than just acknowledging the objective nature of the mismatch. If you assume that the mismatch signals a rejection, or that it means you're a disappointment to your partner, you can easily slip into a cycle like that of Sid and Kate.

You may be reading this and thinking, "How could mismatches in desire possibly be the norm? In a healthy relationship, shouldn't each partner feel desire for the other?" Yes, and the experience of wonderful, mutual desire is exactly what most couples feel as they fall in love at the beginning of their relationships, and for some time afterward. The experience allows plenty of time to come to the conclusion that "when you're truly in love, you both feel equal desire" and its corollary, "if you don't desire one another, you must not be in love."

As life goes on and natural changes in desire occur because of life circumstances or age, these beliefs lead to the assumption that if desire has changed, it's a sign that something is wrong in the relationship. The mismatch is taken to mean rejection, disappointment, or betrayal, and that meaning tees up both partners for a fight. If partners can talk about these feelings in an open way, they can compassionately understand and draw closer to one another. For example, sharing, "I worry that I'm disappointing you," or "I can see that you aren't in the mood as much as you used to be—is it me?" can be a start to sensitively working your way through a mismatch. If you don't talk about your worries, they morph into assumptions and accusations.

One of the most common assumptions is that the mismatch in sexual desire is all about control.

Implied in each of these statements is the idea that the mismatch is happening because one partner is trying to exert control over the other. The fight may then become about whether or not controlling behavior is happening ("You're so controlling!" and "No, I'm not!") or about who is really controlling whom ("Stop controlling me!" and "I'm not controlling *you*, you're controlling *me*!"). Adding the "controlling" labels on top of a mismatch in sexual desire complicates and intensifies the Sex Fight.

So what if we dealt with naturally occurring mismatches differently? What would happen if we accepted that mismatches are just a normal state of affairs and that they don't necessarily hold significant meaning? If Sid and Kate were to accept that their differences in the bedroom are natural, it would give them two options for dealing with their Sex Fight, both of which begin with a joint realization.

Accepting mismatches as an unfortunate reality helps stop the cycle of blaming one another for differences in sexual drive. Both partners acknowledge that a mismatch exists, but the problem is then, "we aren't matching up and that can make things difficult," rather than "the problem is your decreased desire," or "the problem is your overactive desire." Together, you can understand that the challenge actually is, "How do we *deal* with our mismatch?" not, "How do we make our mismatch go away by attempting to change one another?"

With this new joint mindset about the problem, Sid and Kate have two ways of working out their mismatch:

1. Don't talk about the mismatch explicitly, but use it to spice things up.
2. Talk about the mismatch and use empathy to become closer to one another.

OPTION 1: USE THE MISMATCH TO SPICE THINGS UP

For some couples, too much talk about sex spoils the allure and gets in the way of passion. But can you deal with a mismatch without talking a lot about it? In my experience, if a couple can understand that their mismatch is normal and refrain from blaming one another for the problem, they can find some room to actually put a positive spin on the situation. In fact, they might find that the mismatch actually *enhances* their sex life. Here are some ways that Kate and Sid's mismatch could be seen as a positive force between them:

By thinking about their differences in a new light, Sid and Kate actually ignite more excitement between them, meaning the sex might get even better.

OPTION 2: TALK ABOUT THE MISMATCH AND USE EMPATHY TO CONNECT FROM THE CORE

For some couples in a Sex Fight, it helps to have a conversation about the problem, excavating and understanding the complex feelings that lay beneath the fight. The key is for both partners to find and feel empathy for how the mismatch affects their partner.

To resolve the Sex Fight through discussion, it's important to understand the core feelings that are driving the Defense Mode trouble. Just as we saw in the Birthday Fight (see Chapter 6), Kate and Sid's negative cycle is hard to escape because it's driven by painful feelings that are inadvertently reinforced by the other partner: fear, self-doubt, and vulnerability. But those feelings are hard to see on the surface; Sid and Kate would have to excavate under all their defensive actions to find them. Here's what they might be thinking at their cores:

> What is wrong with me that I keep getting rejected? I feel like a loser.

> Maybe there is something seriously wrong with me because my desire seems dead... I feel like a failure.

Both Sid and Kate feel a pang of doubt about themselves because of their Sex Fight, but neither reveals their worries. Whether intentional or not, they've both figured out that it's far safer to keep talking about how the problem is their partner's fault rather than giving their lover more ammunition to blame them for the problem by confessing their insecurities.

Sid pushes away his doubt about his own attractiveness and diverts any blame for their sexual troubles by labeling Kate as the problem: "She's cold." Likewise, Kate pushes away her doubt about her own sexual ability and change in desire by labeling Sid as the problem: "He's pushy." Sid and Kate don't talk about their raw core feelings because it is too risky to reveal their deepest, most painful feelings about the situation in the middle of the fight. It's just easier to blame the other person.

But what if they actually did speak from their cores about their personal difficulties and concerns surrounding the Sex Fight? How would that change the tide? Here's how it might look if Kate decided to speak from her core:

The discussion has changed dramatically. Kate admits that she feels diminished desire and that she worries there's something wrong with her. She also implies that she cares about Sid and therefore she doesn't want to disappoint him. She shows vulnerability and, importantly, she doesn't blame Sid. Her core communication doesn't launch any threats at Sid, so it's easier for him to truly hear what she's saying. When Sid hears Kate speak this honestly and frankly, he has an opportunity to *feel* what the Sex Fight is like for Kate, to see the pain she experiences, and to begin to empathize with that struggle. He also sees more clearly how he unintentionally contributes to her pain, and it becomes more possible to see a way out of the fight.

Here's how it might go if Sid were the first to speak from his core:

Sid openly shares that most of his pain comes from his fear of being rejected. He admits that he worries about his attractiveness to Kate and that he doesn't feel good about his own behavior in the fight. He shares his vulnerable feelings and, importantly, he doesn't blame Kate or throw threats at her, so her guard is down and she can really listen to him. Kate can then see Sid's pain directly, not obscured by defenses, so she can empathize with him and recognize her contribution to the fight.

When a partner admits their fears, worries, and vulnerabilities, that's the moment to empathize and reassure:

* "I know you don't *want* to feel that way."
* "I see why this worries you."
* "I can understand how you feel deprived."
* "Don't worry—I know this is just a temporary issue."
* "I promise I'm not disappointed in you."
* "I get that you're only trying to meet your needs."

Here's what you should *not* do when your partner comes forward with an admission of vulnerability:

> I worry that you don't want me anymore and that I turn you off. I don't want to pressure you, but I just feel so desperate.

> I'm glad you finally admitted it!

> Yeah! It sure is your fault!

> You should feel bad about it!

> So if you feel bad about it, stop pressuring me!

When Kate reacts like this to Sid's expression of his core, she's throwing threats his way, which immediately puts a stop to any Core-to-Core Communication. And Sid is no idiot; with that kind of reaction, he's not likely to risk being vulnerable again. He'll choose to stay in Defense Mode next time, and they'll remain stuck in the fight.

Moments of Core-to-Core Communication are rare and precious, especially when you've been stuck in a fight. When one partner makes a valiant effort to communicate from his or her core, it's a real opportunity to stop a conflict and shouldn't be squandered. But it isn't easy to step out of the habit of Defense Mode communication and follow the other partner into a conversation from the core.

Staying in Core-to-Core Communication starts with having a more compassionate mindset. Sid and Kate can help one another with their respective shame, disappointment, and fears by maintaining an attitude toward one another that focuses on what the other needs most.

Kate would have to set aside her view of Sid as impossible to please and instead hold on to a new understanding: that Sid feels disconnected from her and is pained about it. Sid lets go of his opinion that there's something wrong with Kate and sees instead that Kate feels pressured and demoralized, and that's painful, too.

With these changed mindsets, generous actions can follow.

Whether Kate agrees to sex tonight or not, by keeping a mindset focused on helping Sid feel cared about and not deprived, Kate will communicate that her "no" is *not* a rejection of him as a person. Even if she turns down sex, she still makes it clear that his needs are important to her. Sid can then get the message that "not tonight" is just a statement about her biology or mood in that particular moment, not an overall judgment of him.

With this new mindset, Kate is also likelier to initiate sex more often, because it's now a generous, loving act for her—a way to give freely and to delight Sid—rather than an obligation that underscores she's been failing him. She may not feel *sexual* desire right now, but she does feel desire to *care* about Sid, and that gets her started. It's as if she's saying with her actions, "I know you want more sex, so I'll join you because I love you, even if I don't want it as much myself right now. And who knows? Maybe I'll get more into it once we start." By being generous to Sid, Kate ignites the giving-for-the-sake-of-caring that *she* actually wants in their intimacy, and that carries the chance of helping to make her sexual desire return. To be clear, generously offered physical contact to your partner out of love despite low desire is quite different than "giving in" to pressure or nonconsensual sex. Just giving in and accommodating Sid with an angry mindset behind it is something that Kate's tried before and it doesn't work for either of them.

When Kate has sex with Sid with the mindset that he's impossible to please or out of a sense of obligation, neither of them enjoys it—Sid feels pitied, and Kate feels used.

Similarly, if Sid decides to not pressure Kate but still has the mindset that something is wrong with her, that approach also fails.

Waiting for Kate to initiate while holding the pessimistic mindset that she probably won't ever make the first move leaves Sid still feeling deprived and Kate still feeling Sid's unspoken disappointment and judgment. It's quite a different story if Sid genuinely adopts a mindset that he wants to help Kate feel successful in bed.

Here's how that mindset might lead to more empathetic actions and words in two different scenarios:

SEX TONIGHT   NO SEX TONIGHT

It helps Kate to hear that Sid will be OK with however she's feeling—in the mood or not—without an assumption that "not in the mood" means anything more than that. By accepting "not in the mood" as a flexible state, Sid conveys the message to Kate that she's not a failing, sexless creature who will forever disappoint him. Instead, she's an ordinary human with different levels of sexual desire at different times.

With his new mindset, Sid is open to a different kind of generosity toward Kate: "I know you don't always want sex when I want it, and you hate feeling pressured, so I'll give you some space sometimes, because I love you." *Not having sex* suddenly has generous meaning for Sid—he's stepping away from any pressure *out of love*, giving her what she needs, and that warms the emotional bond between them, setting the stage for better, more generous sex the next time. In addition, Sid doesn't place Kate into the Reputation Lock of being "the person who's never interested in sex" (see the Bad Reputation Fight in Chapter 7 for more on Reputation Locks). He knows that the racy part of Kate's mind is just temporarily switched off. Later, when she does reach out to him sexually, Sid enhances the moment by saying something that recognizes her sexual vitality instead of expressing relief. When both Sid and Kate are mindful of an unhappy core feeling inside the other and make the effort to help eliminate it, the Sex Fight melts away.

To summarize, stopping the Sex Fight means shifting your focus from seeing the other person as the problem and getting curious about the underlying core *feelings* of both partners. By having empathy for your partner's struggle, you gain the ability to change your *mindset* about them and find new ways to give them what they need with an attitude of generosity. This is what truly stops the fight.

A final note: In this chapter, I talk about sex fights, not sexual disorders. By definition, a sexual disorder is a problem that affects the sexual functioning of one partner—low desire, impotence, difficulty with orgasm, or pain during sex are examples. But because sexual disorders cause couples to have less sex, and because they are often hard to understand, they can lead to Sex Fights. Here's how: Once it's clear that there's a difficulty in one partner's sexual functioning, the other partner, out of frustration, may struggle helplessly to somehow make the sexual disorder in their partner go away. Unfortunately, it is so easy for the partner to trip into the potential triggers of a Sex Fight—pressure ("Please get help!"), lack of empathy ("Just get over it!"), blaming or judging ("What's wrong with you?"), or misinterpreting ("This must mean you feel…."). As we saw in this chapter, Kate's low sexual desire led to Sid's frustration with the frequency of sex and then the fight unfolded. By changing the dynamic so that there is more empathy and less pressure, blaming, judgment and misinterpretation, the Sex Fight can be stopped, but Kate's low desire may remain. Healing underlying sexual disorders takes more than stopping the fight that it sparked; it may require medical intervention, sex therapy, or psychotherapy.

THE SEX FIGHT TOOLBOX

 When you ask for changes in your sex life, avoid messages that convey judgment of your partner.

 Stop the mutual blame.

 Understand the core feelings hiding underneath Defense Mode and find compassion for your partner's core.

 Keep your mindset focused on what your partner needs most at his or her core.

 Lighten up on expectation and evaluation, which only lead to more dissatisfaction and judgment, the engines of the Sex Fight.

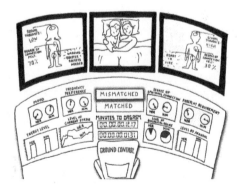 Assume that mismatches *will* happen and realize that you have a choice about how to interpret them—you can even spin them for the better.

CHAPTER 12

THE
DIFFICULT RELATIVES
FIGHT

THE DIFFICULT RELATIVES FIGHT CAN be a particularly challenging conflict for couples. After all, it's loved ones who you're dealing with, whether they're your partner's relatives or your own. If you can't agree on how to deal with family—on how generous to be with them or how much time to spend with them, or how to interact with them—tension will build and arguments will break out.

These fights can seem impossible to solve, and they can grow worse over time. Let's look at an example of one of the most classically challenging situations: the difficult mother-in-law.

Paul has always been close with his family. When he married Carin, there was a little bit of friction between Carin and his mother about wedding plans and such, but he optimistically assumed that it was just related to the stress they both felt with the details of planning the event. But it's been four years now, and nothing has gotten better between them; in fact, it's gotten worse. Paul always feels like he's in the middle. He knows his mother has some strong opinions, but Carin seems to get unnecessarily irked at everything his mother does. It's not easy to deal with his mother complaining about Carin, but Carin doesn't have to make it worse. When he wants to visit his mom, he already knows the face Carin will make about it, so lately he's taken to visiting her alone. And then, when he comes back from the visit, Carin is usually in a crabby mood and makes sarcastic remarks about "running home to Mommy." He's so frustrated with Carin—she could show a little more respect.

Carin has had it with Paul's mother. Joan is the most controlling person she has ever met—she's always giving her opinion about matters that should be between just Paul and Carin. She weighed in on which apartment they rented, the way they ought to set it up, and lately Joan seems to think she's the expert on how they should raise their son. In her view, Paul is obviously used to being controlled by his mother, so he doesn't even notice it's happening. Carin tried at first to be civil to Joan, but that was before she had to endure waves and waves of Joan's opinions and criticism over the years. She's furious with Paul for letting his mother be so involved in their lives and hates competing for his attention with her mother-in-law. It all seems so cliché and foolish, but she can't help but feel that way.

WHY THE DIFFICULT RELATIVES FIGHT IS HARD TO STOP

1. You can't agree on what the problem actually is.

One big reason it's so difficult to break free from this fight is that Carin and Paul each have very different views of what the problem actually is. To Paul, the problem is obvious: He's being fought over. The more he tries to do what his wife wants, the more he feels like he's betraying his mother; the more he tries to be kind to his mother, the more Carin makes him feel like he's betraying her. In his mind, the situation looks like this, and it's mostly Carin's fault:

Carin sees things very differently. It's obvious to her that Paul's mother is way too attached to her adult son—maybe even pathologically so. And Paul doesn't do anything to inform her that he's no longer five years old and that she can back off. To Carin, the situation looks like this, and it's mostly Paul's fault:

When Carin presents her view of the fight to Paul, he dismisses it because it seems so ridiculously wrong to him. And Carin feels the same way about Paul's point of view. *Complicating factor number one: different perspectives about the problem.*

2. You hold opposite views regarding the difficult relative.

Carin and Paul also each have completely different views on Paul's mother, Joan.

Carin's view of Joan is mostly negative—everything about her mother-in-law is annoying: She's controlling, interfering, nosy, clingy, sneaky, and paranoid. Even when Joan does something nice, like the time she babysat their son for a weekend so Carin and Paul could get away, Carin sensed that there was something manipulative about it—either she was trying to rack up "points" so that later on she could talk endlessly about how much better she cares for the baby than Carin does, or she was trying to tie herself even more tightly to Paul by making him feel indebted to her.

Paul's view of his mother is quite the opposite. He knows his mother isn't perfect, but he also knows that she means well, and he loves her. When Joan does something annoying, he knows that her intentions are still good, and when she does something generous, it's genuine.

" Ok, she's not perfect, but she's not all that bad ... "

" Are you kidding? She does this, this, this ... "

Recognize the pattern? Paul and Carin are *polarized* in their view of Joan. Paul sees all the positives about his mother, and Carin sees all the negatives. The more tenaciously he recites the positives, such as "she's not so bad," or "she's a good person who really does mean well," the more forcefully Carin will list the evidence of her past offenses. The more Carin contends that "she's just wrong," or "she has a lot of nerve," or "she doesn't know her place," the more Paul will insist that she's blowing it out of proportion. Neither is able to convince the other to change their opinion, and they stay stuck. As time goes on, they become increasingly fixed in the way they view the situation with

Paul's mother. *Complicating factor number two: opposing, polarized mindsets about Joan.*

3. There is a Reputation Lock between the relative and the non-related partner.

As Carin's negative feelings about Paul's mother harden into place, Joan becomes more fixed in her mindset as well. Over time, in her frequent fighting with Carin, Joan develops a very negative view of her son's partner. To her, Carin is cold, overcontrolling, unwelcoming, and always angry and pouty. Joan has wondered more than once whether Paul made the right choice in Carin. How could he love someone like that? You can imagine Carin's and Joan's thought bubbles when they have to be together:

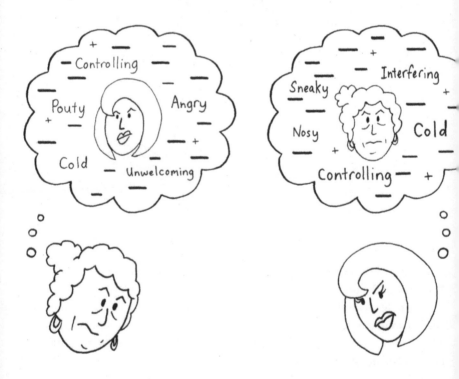

Carin and Joan see one another with fixed negative reputations; the mother-in-law and daughter-in-law are stuck in Reputation Lock with one another, and neither is making any effort to change that. (See the Bad Reputation Fight in Chapter 7 for more on Reputation Lock.) *Complicating factor number three: locked Bad Reputations.*

REPUTATION LOCK

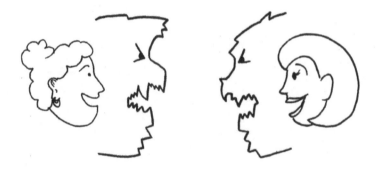

MINDSET MATTERS

If you understand the extent to which negative mindsets drive the Difficult Relative Fight, you can begin to see the way to stopping it.

Here's a fact about fights: The more tightly you hold on to a negative or judgmental mindset about another person, the less likely it is that you'll be able to resolve a fight with that person. Fights that become impossible to solve are those in which the thought bubbles above the parties' heads are filled with all negatives and no positives.

Holding a completely negative view of another person is the same as having a solid Reputation Lock on him or her. The judgmental attitude has such a hold on you that you can no longer find your way back to a mindset that's not combative. Why do negative mindsets matter so much? Because they change the way you take in new information, they change the way you behave, and as we will see, they "leak."

NEGATIVE MINDSETS EAT UP POSITIVE EVENTS . . .

Imagine Carin's thought bubble floating over her head, full of negatives whenever she thinks about Joan. When Joan buys a nice gift for Carin, how does Carin think about that gift? Is it, "Oh, how lovely! Thank you!" or is it, "What's this about? Is she about to ask for something?" Carin's negative mindset will suck any positive action right up, call it fake, suspicious, or an anomaly. The thoughtful gesture doesn't change the cloud of negativity at all, and Joan will go away thinking that even when she tries to be nice to Carin it doesn't work.

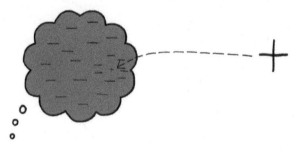

. . . AND NEGATIVE MINDSETS WELCOME NEW NEGATIVE EVENTS

Imagine that Joan calls the house, and when Carin picks up the phone, Joan says, "May I please speak to Paul?" Will Carin think, "Oh, she must have something urgent to discuss with Paul, and that's why she didn't say hello to me" or, "What kind of person calls and doesn't even have the courtesy to say hello to the person who picks up the phone?" With the negative thought bubble about Joan over her head, this slightly negative interaction seems to prove that Carin's opinion of Joan is *so true*, and she'll probably share the story with Paul later: "Can you believe how rude she is?!"

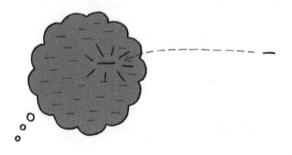

Negative mindsets welcome and treasure new negative events and use them to strengthen the belief that "what I always thought about him or her is true." Positive events don't stand a chance of surviving in that dark cloud. Once Carin and Joan have developed negative mindsets about one another and locked the other into a Bad Reputation, any positive interaction between them will get spun in an unfavorable light by both parties.

NEGATIVE MINDSETS BREED NEGATIVE INTERACTIONS

Thoughts drive actions. If Carin believes that Joan is always intrusive, Carin will behave in ways that try to stop Joan from intruding, perhaps by not telling her things or by keeping her distance. If Joan believes that Carin is always cold, Joan might try to "warm her up" by finding ways to get involved in Carin's life, or she might stop trying to get closer to Carin and instead invest more of her energy in being close to Paul. Carin might then reasonably feel Joan's behavior is even more of an intrusion or out-of-line. Since they choose their actions in response to the negative mindsets they hold, negative interactions continue to happen and build up.

NEGATIVE MINDSETS LEAK

Most people have a sense that negative mindsets tend to lead to negative interactions, so we work hard to not let our judgment of others show. Unfortunately, that often doesn't work too well. Here's why: Suppose Rick believes that Patrick, his neighbor, is a real *jerk*. There are so many unneighborly things that Patrick has done, and Rick is pretty locked in his negative mindset about Patrick. When they leave their house every morning to retrieve the newspapers from their respective doorsteps and cheerily wish one another a good morning, do either of them actually believe that the other wishes

them a genuinely good morning? Is it possible for them to completely hide how they really feel about one another?

Most of us believe that with the exception of certain special cases like the neighbor we don't care about anyway, we're pretty good at keeping a poker face concerning our negative views of others. Yet most of us can also tell when someone is acting outwardly friendly but actually doesn't like us at all. You get that feeling—something doesn't match between the words and the body language, or between the words and the tone of voice, and you just *know* not to trust the words. If we're all so good at concealing our negative thoughts about others, but we're also all so good at detecting what isn't genuine, we have to face the fact that what we feel *leaks,* and its visible to others. We leak our judgments, our criticisms, and our negative mindsets.

If you intuit that someone doesn't like you, you'll likely walk away from that interaction feeling that you don't like them either; that's human nature. (The opposite is true as well—we tend to like people who we sense like us.)

When Joan and Carin are together, they may try to act civilly toward one another, but they still hang on to their negative views of one another, and that leaks out.

Unintentionally, Joan leaks that she sees Carin as cold and unwelcoming, and Carin leaks that she thinks Joan is intrusive. They almost don't pay attention to the "civil" conversation, because the leaks are much more telling. As they watch one another's mismatched tone of voice or revealing body language, they feel more animosity toward the other, and it poisons the interaction even more. They both walk away feeling unfairly disliked and therefore feel even less love and respect for one another.

In sum, negative mindsets keep fights going and make them worse, and not just between mothers-in-law and daughters-in-laws. It's the same between partners. Just as with the Bad Reputation Fight (see Chapter 7), if you and your partner hold negative views of one another, or anyone either of you care deeply about, you'll explain away positive gestures, focus on the new negative interactions between you, act judgmentally and critically toward one another, and, even when you try to be nice, leak your true negative feelings.

How often do partners say, "I'll change when I see my partner change," while hanging on to a negative mindset about their partner? "Just start to show me that you're more giving; I'll believe it when I see it," they say, and you can almost picture them tapping their foot, laying out the test, waiting to be proven wrong but pessimistically expecting to be proven right. With a negative mindset, you won't see the change, or you won't count it!

You can imagine how this plays out in some of the fights we've explored in past chapters: Ed tries to be better at celebrating Sara's birthday, but instead of seeing the effort Ed put in to make her cake, Sara saw the mess he made. Sam wouldn't notice if Molly made an effort to spend less this month; it wouldn't be enough to change how he thinks of her. With a leaking negative mindset, your

268 * STOP THE FIGHT!

"attempts to change" aren't all that believable. Saying she appreciates that Maxine bought groceries doesn't ring true if Jeanette leaks her annoyance that Maxine doesn't do much around the house.

Some people believe that they can solve the problem of leaking their negative mindsets by just developing a better poker face. "I'll just conceal it better, and then I can't be blamed for contributing to the poor interaction." Perhaps that could work with the unneighborly neighbor, but your partner and close relatives and friends usually know you too well, and somehow they just *sense* that something negative lurks in your thoughts. Mindsets matter, and only by changing negative mindsets can you actually stop the fight and change the interaction for the better.

STOP THE FIGHT BY STOPPING NEGATIVE MINDSETS

The Difficult Relatives Fight has two types of mindset problems that sustain the fight. First, Paul and Carin are polarized in their respective views of Joan, so they can't reach a resolution on how to frame their relationship with her. Second, Joan's and Carin's negative mindsets about one another guarantee continual negative interactions between them. To stop the fight, all mindsets need to shift to change the interaction. Fortunately, shifting just one of them at first can eventually help shift them all.

PAUL'S AND CARIN'S MINDSETS

Remember how differently Paul and Carin see the situation with Paul's mother?

They're both angry about how the other interacts with Joan: Paul is annoyed that Carin won't get along with her, and Carin is aggravated that Paul seems too attached to Joan. To stop the fight, Paul and Carin have to shift their attention away from Joan and more to one another, and work to understand the dilemma that each one is struggling with. Understanding your partner's dilemma means working together to see what their core feelings are about the problem. It helps a lot to also know something about their life history and how it influences their view of the problem. Then, you can begin to recognize the threats that your partner is responding to that cause him or her to behave in Defense Mode.

WHAT'S MY PARTNER'S DILEMMA? CORES, HISTORIES, VULNERABILITIES, AND THREATS

Here's what Carin might be able to understand about Paul's dilemma:

Paul's Core: Paul loves both his mother and his wife and wants to find a way to keep a relationship with his mother without it destroying his marriage. Family is important to him, and he wants to keep a connection to his parents over their lifetimes. Paul knows his mother can be difficult at times, but he loves her and doesn't want to hurt her. He feels his mother's disappointment in him very acutely and doesn't want to be the cause of her pain. But he doesn't want to hurt Carin either. He wishes he could be the one who could bring them together, but he can't seem to make it happen. At the core, he feels such a longing for a way to succeed at keeping everyone he loves happy.

Paul's History and Vulnerability: For Paul, detaching entirely from his mother has been difficult, even before he was married. Throughout his life his mother has always found a way to make him feel uncomfortable if he didn't do what she wanted, and he has a hard time standing up to people in general. He knows it isn't one of his best qualities, but his way of dealing with his mother's controlling behavior in the past has been to just give in, and he's been doing it for so long that it feels normal to him. In his heart of hearts, though, he knows his mother can be intrusive, but he wouldn't dare reveal that to Carin. It seems too likely she would then pressure him even harder to distance himself from his mother, and that's fraught with challenges for him. So, instead, he vehemently disagrees with Carin's view of his mother.

Paul's Threats: When Carin constantly reminds him that he should stand up to his mother, Paul pushes back because he doesn't want to hurt his mother *and* because Carin's critique makes him feel even worse about not standing up to her. He truly feels caught: If he acts to stop Carin's criticism, he'll be hurting his mother, and if he tries to avoid hurting his mother, he'll get even more criticism from Carin. As we can see, some threats Paul feels come from the current situation with Carin, and some threats bear a shadow of history in them.

Here's what Paul might be able to understand about Carin's dilemma:

Carin's Core: Carin's idea of marriage is that it's about a couple being devoted to one another, a relationship in which each partner is uniquely special to the other. Carin wants to build a home and a life that the two of them can lead together, without the influence of outsiders. It doesn't seem right that outsiders get a vote in what the couple does. Carin longs for a feeling of deep connection with Paul, and the battle with his mother makes that wish seem so painfully out of reach.

THE DIFFICULT RELATIVES FIGHT * 271

Carin's History and Vulnerabilities: At times, Carin feels unsure of being loved, although she thought that she dealt with that insecurity a long time ago. She was competitive with her older brother growing up and felt he was more loved in the family than she was. This situation with Paul and his mother makes those uncomfortable feelings bubble up again—it feels like Paul is choosing his mother over her.

Carin's Threats: To Carin, Paul's mother's desire to be involved in so much of their lives feels intrusive, and every time Joan does something, Carin views it through that lens: "Joan is competing with me for Paul's love." It doesn't help that Joan is critical, too. However annoying it is, though, Carin knows she could probably let it roll off if Joan just gave them more space.

The most frustrating thing is that all the conflict with his mother creates tension between her and Paul, which interferes with one of Carin's most cherished values—that the bond between a couple be special and strong. Carin feels truly stuck because no matter what, the bond she wants with Paul is threatened; either she loses the specialness by giving in and sharing him with his mother, or she loses the peace and strength of their connection by continuing to fight with him about his mother. Neither approach works. Carin is desperately trying to fight off the multiple threats she experiences, some of which come from the current situation between her and Paul, and some of which come with the shadow of her past history.

What if Paul and Carin could talk to one another from the core so that they were both able to acknowledge and understand the other's difficult dilemma and be compassionate toward it? Carin would see how hard it is for Paul to set boundaries with his mother, and she'd no longer blame him for it. She would understand that it's always been hard for him and that it will be a learning process for him to change. Paul would see how sensitive Carin is to feeling competitive about love, and then he wouldn't blame her for it; it's a vulnerability she has, and it will be a learning process for her to completely trust Paul's love for her.

When they each realize the dilemma their partner has, it becomes understandable *why* their partner came up with the solution they'd been arguing for all along. Carin's dilemma makes her propose that they "set limits" with Paul's mother, keeping her far away from the tightly bounded space they have as a couple. Paul's dilemma makes him repeatedly insist that he and Carin can have a close relationship even with his mother nearby.

Paul's Wish

Carin's Wish

With full awareness of, and compassion for, one another's respective dilemmas (cores, histories, vulnerabilities, and threats), and a new understanding of what they each desire in their interactions with their relatives, Paul and Carin will be better able to find a compromise that works to actually stop this fight. But they also need to do something about the polarized mindsets they have toward one another and toward Joan.

RESOLVING POLARIZED MINDSETS IN THE DIFFICULT RELATIVES FIGHT

Because of Paul and Carin's core feelings about the situation, they each express their opinions about Joan in terms of two important values that have become polarized: Carin has become the flag-bearer for the couple's bond and Paul has become the ambassador for family loyalty. Paul and Carin fight about Joan because how they relate to her connects directly to these two values.

When understood in this way, we can see that both Paul and Carin are trying to do something good about values that really matter to them. Since Paul places such high importance on family loyalty, he's able to see Joan in a positive light and pass off her annoying behaviors as "not so bad." Carin, who places a high importance on the special bond between a couple, believes that Joan's behavior creates problems because she's interfering in Carin and Paul's relationship.

The two values they're each individually advocating for are, in fact, *shared*. Quite likely, both can agree that loyalty to your family is a good thing, and both can agree that there should be a special bond between a couple. When Carin and Paul start solving for both values at the same time, and not just one or the other, a solution to their fight becomes possible.

So what do solutions that take into account both the values of family loyalty and a special couple bond look like in real life?

Suppose Joan calls and says she's coming over to bring a special dinner she's cooked to eat together. Paul hears the request and thinks about how he can respond in a way that won't be a threat to Carin, is sensitive to what he knows is core for Carin and will also show loyalty to his family. He tells his mother he'll call back to let her know if that works for them, and then he consults with Carin. When she hears about the invitation, Carin understands the dilemma Paul is in; she doesn't criticize his mother or him, and she lets him know she appreciates how hard it was for him to put his mother on hold and not say yes right away.

They come up with a solution that addresses both sharing time with Joan (the value of family loyalty), but also builds in some special time for the two of them (the value of the couple bond). Paul calls his mother back and tells her, "We would love to have dinner with you and we know we'll enjoy what you cooked. Would you be able to stay for a while after dinner to watch Joey so Carin and I can go out for a bit?" This resolution is powered by their effort to not inadvertently trigger threats and by the positive mindsets that Carin and Paul work to cultivate about one another: full of compassion for the core feelings and vulnerabilities that each partner brings to the fight.

CHANGING CARIN'S AND JOAN'S MINDSETS

There is just one more pair of mindset changes that could make this fight stop for good. Carin and Joan have built up some major negative thought bubbles about one another that need to be scrubbed. Since negative mindsets (aka Reputation Lock) perpetuate fights, and positive actions typically don't do enough to shift a negative mindset, somehow Carin and Joan have to figure out a way to change their attitudes toward one another. If only they could get rid of the negatives and let in the positives.

So how does a person just stop thinking that they don't like their mother-in-law? That's got to be impossible! You might agree that Carin holds a negative mindset about her mother-in-law for very good reasons, or that Joan doesn't deserve to be given the benefit of the doubt. But consider this: Until Carin can release her locked negative mindset about Joan, Joan's negative mindset about Carin will also stay locked. Both of them will be stuck in the Bad Reputation Fight (see Chapter 7). Carin can easily say that the mindset Joan holds about her simply isn't true—Carin isn't really "a stubborn, cold person who wants to shut Joan out," but Joan persists in believing it. If only Joan could understand the *truth*: Carin would love to have a good relationship with Joan and only feels the need to set limits on her mother-in-law's involvement because Joan oversteps her role.

If Carin sees that Joan's mindset about her is so mistaken, can she also see that her own mindset about Joan is probably mistaken as well? While it seems to Carin that Joan clings to being the most important woman in Paul's life and doesn't want to let him have a normal relationship with his wife, the truth may be that Joan wants to have a good relationship with both Paul *and* Carin but senses rejection from Carin, and feels she has to push harder in the face of Carin's resistance in order to see Paul and the kids at all. If Carin keeps leaking an attitude of "rejection" toward Joan, and Joan keeps leaking an inclination to "clinging," both will continue their negative actions, further entrenching the negative mindsets. So, the first step in changing a negative mindset to a more positive one is to realize that what you assume to be true is likely not the whole truth. Drop your negative assumptions and search for more information.

Step 1: Change Mindset

This is certainly not an easy thing to do, but it's important to set your intentions to *try* to change your negative mindset about the other person.

The best path to understanding behavior you don't like is to assume that the unpleasant behavior comes from someone's Defense Mode, not from his or her core. What do we know about Defense Mode behavior? It's always triggered by a threat. Take Joan's clinginess, for example. Why would a person feel the need to cling to someone else? What are the primary threats to most humans' feelings that would cause them to cling to another person? It's usually caused by fears of feeling rejected, irrelevant, or abandoned.

Step 2: What's Her Threat?

If Carin can recognize that Joan feels those threats, she's also likely to recognize that Joan's feelings makes some sense, especially given how Carin has acted toward Joan in the past. Carin realizes that she's played a part in triggering Joan's clingy behavior and knows what she can do to help make it stop: Act in a manner that helps Joan feel less threatened by her. That might mean making an effort to come across as the opposite of controlling, cold, and unwelcoming, or it might mean engaging in a watershed conversation acknowledging her own bad impact on Joan.

For Carin to be able to act with a more positive mindset about her mother-in-law, she'd have to take some time to consider what Joan's core really is, what her vulnerabilities are, and to understand what Joan wants most from her relationship with Carin and Paul.

Step 3: What's Her Core?

Loves Paul
Cares about us
CORE
Fear of losing closeness
with Paul
Imperfect

When Carin reflects on the situation, she might come to realize that all Joan wants is to keep a connection with her son. No matter how misguided Joan is in showing it, that's likely the true core of what she wants. She has her own vulnerabilities, of course. Joan likely overinvests in the relationship with her son for some good reasons that Carin may not yet understand. Joan may have never had to rethink her focus on Paul before, and she's understandably scared. Carin does see that it must be hard for Joan to have so little support in her life, and suddenly she finds some compassion for her mother-in-law.

Once Carin has altered her mindset about Joan to a positive one, her more favorable attitude will leak out in her interactions with Joan. Even if Joan doesn't go through this same mindset scrub regarding her feelings about Carin, inevitably, as their interactions become more positive and productive, Joan will come away realizing that she's been mistaken about Carin's Bad Reputation. Since she no longer feels as rejected by Carin, Joan develops a more approving view of her, and her mindset begins to change as well. And as we have seen, when the mindsets change, the fight stops.

Hold it, you say—it seems like Carin has to do the most work here . . . how is that fair? Doesn't Joan hold at least half of the responsibility for this conflict? Yes, Joan clearly contributes to the fight, too, but either one of them can start the process of ending it. Out of pride and a desire not to "give in," people sometimes choose to keep a fight going. Sometimes we even believe that by holding out and not conceding to anything, the other person may eventually realize the wrongs of their ways and apologize, or that somehow we'll "win" or be proven right in the end.

Everyone has heard horrible tales of custody battles between divorcing parents who fight to the bitter end in court, ironically creating more misery for their children, all in the name of being proven the better parent. At some point, hopefully they recognize that their children will be better off if they just stop the fight. This is Carin's choice as well; it's not between "giving in" to Joan and "winning," but between keeping the fight going and stopping it. It doesn't matter who begins the process of stopping the fight—either party involved can decide to start making changes—but choosing to do nothing keeps the fight going.

Mindset that keeps the fight going

In contrast, here's a fight-stopping mindset:

Mindset that prepares to stop the figh⊦

Each one of these thoughts creates openings in the cloud of conflict:

* Go out on a limb and make the assumption that the other person has good intentions
* Take responsibility for your own actions
* Recognize that you may not be seeing the Big Picture View—you might be missing something
* Learn more about the other person's core so that you can empathize with their struggle, too
* Reach for a better understanding rather than just making assumptions that confirm previous negative mindsets.

In Carin and Paul's Difficult Relative Fight, Carin could choose to insist that she's right about Paul being a "Mama's boy," and Paul could insist that Carin is wrong to freeze out his mother, but those choices perpetuate the conflict and just make the fight worse over time. So the question is: Keep it going or stop the fight? You can choose to end the fight by choosing to have a fight-stopping mindset.

THE DIFFICULT RELATIVES TOOLBOX

 Difficult Relative Fights stay stuck because of fixed, polarized mindsets.

 Negative mindsets are resistant to change by positive events and love new negative events. Negative feelings leak into the interaction with the difficult relative, making the fight grow worse over time.

Come back from polarization and reconnect about the shared key values in the Difficult Relative Fight.

Understand the complexity of your partner's dilemma—their core, history, threat, and Defense Mode.

Choose to have a mindset that will lead you to stop the fight.

THE BIG PICTURE

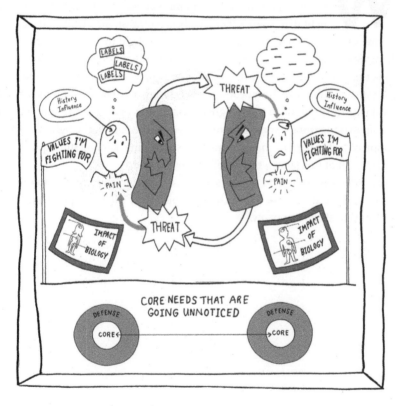

WHEN I MEET A COUPLE for the first time in my practice, I see them at a moment of maximum anguish. Whatever the unique fight that plagues them, it's been going on for a while. The length of time varies, of course, but for every couple, the fight that brings them into a therapist's office has been going on long enough that both partners have lost hope that it can stop. It's not surprising that people lose hope. Think about it: The same argument keeps repeating, and nothing ever changes. All the efforts you make to try to move toward greater happiness or to end the conflict just end up making things worse. So now you've got the pain of the fight, the frustration of trying hard to change it and not succeeding, and the subsequent loss of hope. All of this takes a major toll on your mood.

But what can be hard to notice is the toll it takes on your vision. After living under fight conditions for a long time, the picture of what's happening in your relationship starts to narrow.

THE PAIN PICTURE
(aka The Little Picture)

What you feel most strongly is how much pain you're in, and what you see most clearly is *who* is causing you to feel that way. You see the flaws and nasty actions of your partner with incredible acuity, and you see absolutely clearly how it affects you.

The more pain the fight causes you, the more the picture zooms in to be all about your partner. You can't help it, really; pain changes your focus completely. When you're in pain, all you can think about is making it stop. If it's a toothache, you can forget about work or doing anything enjoyable—it's all tooth, all the time.

If it's your partner who's causing you pain, you end up focusing more and more on getting him or her to stop. "Just stop, already!" is what we want to scream.

When a couple first comes to me, both partners are suffering, so both have a fairly focused vision on the Little Picture—their individual Pain Pictures. What amazes me, every time, is what happens when we start to zoom out and see the Big Picture.

THE BIG PICTURE

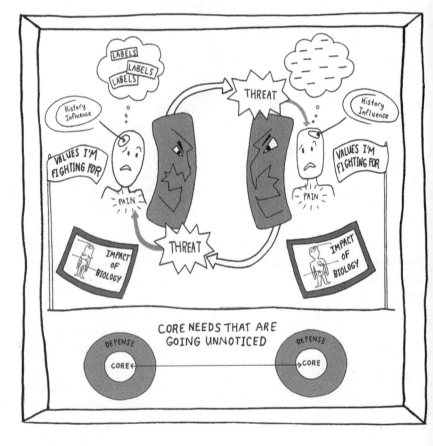

Seeing the Big Picture is about seeing the connection between your pain and your partner's pain. It's realizing the connection between the threats you each perceive, the defenses you each use, and how those defensive actions pain your partner. It's acknowledging how you each contribute to what's happening and how you label one another's behavior. It's recognizing how your history and your partner's history make you each extra sensitive to certain types of pain. It's knowing you have innate differences and working with the mismatch. It's understanding the values that you're fighting for and jointly holding them. It's figuring out how things escalate and choosing to prevent them together. And most importantly, the Big Picture is about understanding and empathizing with what is core for both you and your partner.

With couples in my practice, once we start examining all the features of the Big Picture, things start to change. Couples see what they haven't seen before— they see a path to change, and hope returns. For me, personally, experiencing those moments of hope, when a loving connection again seems possible, is what keeps me doing this work.

As humans in relationships, most of us end up fighting the very same fights. And the Big Pictures are often similar. My wish in writing this book was to share all the Big Pictures that I kept uncovering over and over with my clients, so that couples everywhere who fight these same fights could have the chance to zoom out their focus and find hope, too.

With hope, change becomes possible. And with a clear Big Picture, you have a map for rebuilding your connection. As a couple looks at the Big Picture of their fight with understanding, compassion, and empathy, the fight begins to melt away. It's a process that takes work from both partners, but that work can't begin if both partners just see their own individual Pain Picture. The small Pain Picture View suggests a one-sided and usually unlikely change, in which your partner is the only one who has to do something differently to stop your pain. The Big Picture View makes it clear that real change in a relationship can only happen when, like a bridge, the connection between partners is rebuilt from both sides.

Rebuilding a bridge as a couple goes beyond stopping the fights. As you stop your fights, you begin to see one another's core much more vividly. You open yourself more; you risk being vulnerable together again. When you see openness and vulnerability in your partner, your empathy and compassion for one another blossoms. The more times you create a positive cycle of responsiveness together, the more attached you feel and the stronger your bond with each other.

My deepest hope is that you and your partner can use this book as a blueprint to begin the process of rebuilding your own bridge to a relationship that lasts.

TERMS USED IN *STOP THE FIGHT!*

The following terms appear in the order they are introduced in the book.

Core: The real you, with your strengths and vulnerabilities, your good intentions and your most genuine feelings. Your core feelings include what you long for, what you worry about, and what you need as well as your hopes and fears about your relationship with your partner.

Core Mode: The mode of action that comes directly from your core: acting on your core feelings. When you are in Core Mode you can be open, flexible, generous, vulnerable, and brave. For example, you are in Core Mode when you express the caring that you feel or the fears you feel *directly*, without simultaneously protecting yourself. When you are able to speak or act with vulnerability, you are in Core Mode.

Defense Mode: The mode of action that is self-protective in the face of threats: taking actions that lessen pain by fight or flight. Defense Mode is normal and automatic and is the logical mode to be in when under threat, but the actions taken in Defense Mode frequently have a negative impact on partners. As both partners keep defending themselves, they inadvertently put out threats that trigger each other. Fights keep happening when both partners get stuck in Defense Mode and have trouble returning to Core Mode.

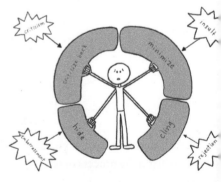

Threats: Something that occurs around you that puts you at risk for feeling hurt or disconnected. In fights between couples, common threats are events that cause you to feel criticized, controlled, misunderstood, abandoned, or disrespected. Threats trigger you to go into Defense Mode, taking you away from your core.

Defense Mode Actions: The actions you take when in Defense Mode. There are a wide variety of actions people do when in Defense Mode and everyone has their favorites. Some examples are: tuning out, pressuring, criticizing back, avoiding, or complaining.

Just buy gifts to apologize.

Distance sexually.

Brush the fight under the rug for now.

Drink more to stop thinking about the problem.

Say point louder and firmer to make sure you get it.

Deny responsibility.

Stay at work because it is less stressful than home.

Leave a mess to show how much worse I could be.

Avoid you when you're angry.

Tune you out.

Tell you what I think you want to hear.

Watch TV.

Stop talking to avoid saying anything wrong.

Pick apart your arguments to show how you are wrong.

Take it out on the kids.

Remind you how this isn't the first time.

Push harder to connect with you.

Criticize back.

Resentfully, just do it myself.

Tell you again how you misunderstood me.

Explain why I didn't do what I said I would.

Make a joke to lighten the situation.

Hide my feelings.

Leave the room in the middle of a fight.

Spend money to take my mind off things.

Core-to-Core Communication: A form of communication between couples where both partners speak from their core. In Core-to-Core Communication, couples express their deepest feelings and vulnerabilities and say directly what they need from one another without threat.

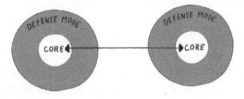

Defense–Core Error: The tendency to mistakenly view defensive behavior that happens in response to threats as core to your partner's personality. As a result, we begin to interact with the partner as if the good, well-meaning core isn't there anymore. We can clearly see in ourselves that there is a big difference between who we are under stress or threat and who we are at the core. But when observing others, we are more likely to see Defense Mode behavior as intrinsic to who the other person is, making the Defense–Core Error.

Reputation Lock: When both partners stay in Defense Mode with each other for a long time and they no longer flex in and out of Core Mode, partners begin to think of one another in a fixed way with Locked Reputations. Reputation Lock is what happens when both parties repeatedly make the Defense–Core Error until they no longer can see their partner's core.

ACKNOWLEDGMENTS

I**T FEELS ALMOST MIRACULOUS TO** witness couples finding their way back from bitterly entrenched, truly desperate fights to the marvel of peace. When a new insight or innovative way to think about a problem made all the difference, when couples could deeply see each other's pain again, comfort one another, and feel the love return, with hope renewed.

So, first, I want to thank my clients. It was in those moments with you that the ideas, metaphors, and images in this book were inspired. Thank you for your trust and for showing me, and in turn the readers of this book, what drives all of us into these universal, circular fights and what can be done to help us out of them.

This book has always been about the illustrations; my vision was to collect all the drawings I had scribbled out while working with couples over the years and find a way to share them more broadly. But the scribbles needed Emily Tomasik, who turned them into the wonderful illustrations you see here. Emily has been a true partner in creating this book. I am deeply appreciative of her artistic talent, patience, reliability, intuitive awareness of people, and willing-ness to always go the extra mile to make an image just a little more precise, expressive, or zany. I am so grateful that we found each other and I have enjoyed every minute of working together. Thank you!

Stop the Fight! is a culmination of the wisdom I have learned through the various avenues of my career as a psychologist and an executive coach. As such, there have been many who have influenced me along the way whom I consider my teachers and mentors. Thank you to Dodi Tobin, Alice Powers, Leigh McCullough, Tim Walsh, Judith Jordan, Carolyn Maltus, Joe Shay, Lois Eichler, Dina Hirshfeld, Robin Masheb, John Mehm, Rosa Ament, Lauren Saler, Andrea Winters, Iris Bagwell, Phil McArthur, Bob Putnam, Rena Fredman, Suzie Marder, my colleagues at the Exetor Group, Deborah Wayne, Ted Miller, George Faller, and Sue Johnson.

To my friends, family, and colleagues who read drafts and offered input or professional advice, and thereby provided so much support for me and for this project. Thanks especially to Adrienne Alexander, Rebecca Amaru, Michelle Avigan, Alexis Berkowitz, Frances Blumenfeld, Juli Brasch, Rachel Brody, Alice Canale, Amy Chua, Jennifer DeCamp, George Faller, Tamar Feder, Jaime Feit, Susan Birke Fiedler, Rena Fredman, Lisa Gilbert, Michah Gottlieb, Norma Grill, Laurie Hoffman, Suzanne Iasenza, Sue Johnson, Gina Kaiser, Marty Klein, Devorah Kosowsky, Josh Kosowsky, David Kriegel, Lois Lustig, Liz Marcus, Yuval Marcus, Suzie Marder, Tom Martin, Sharon Oran, Ilana Rosenberg, Lauren Saler, Adina Shoulson, Lara Siegel, Marisa Stadtmauer, Dana Tangir, Andrea Viders, Barbara Weiner, and Ilene Zwirn.

The final stewards of this book have been three fantastic women: my agent, Jessica Papin at Dystel and Goderich, and my editors, Sasha Tropp and Allie Bochicchio at The Experiment. I am grateful for your enthusiasm for this book and your belief in its mission. There would have been much more to edit if not for my amazing friend, Lisa Kahn, who carefully read every word of the book, thought through every idea, and made the book infinitely more readable. I so appreciate your friendship and your dedication and excitement about the book.

To my wonderful parents, Marsha and Peter Brody, my sisters, aunt, nieces, nephews, and mothers-, fathers-, sister-, and brothers-in-law. Thank you for your encouragement of this book and all my endeavors.

To my three sweeties, Eva, Jesse, and Lev. Your support of this book has been so important to me. Those moments when you proudly showed chapters to your friends, offered input about the illustrations, or said, "Maybe this will help me with my partner someday!" were better than just about anything. I spend so much of my time feeling proud of the three of you; it's quite a trip to feel your pride in me.

And finally, to my partner of twenty-five years: Hal, you have been everything to me—everything I could ever imagine I could want. But since we're talking about the book here, let me cover all of *those* things. We, too, have had many of these fights at one time or another, and I've learned so much from our experiences and how we've struggled to sort issues out with one another. You've read the whole thing, you've *lived* the whole thing, and you've been incredibly encouraging and supportive all the way through. I am so, so grateful for you.

INDEX

Page numbers in *italics* indicate
   illustrations.

actions, *120*, 120–21, 126
   See also Defense Mode Actions
advice, 4–5, *5*, 11–15, *12*, *14*
appreciation, 10, *74*, 74–75
arrows, current, 42, *42*
assumptions, 225–26, 235–40,
   236–37, *239*
awareness, 107–10

Bad Reputation Fight, 113–34
   about, 114
   defensive actions, buildup of,
      115–17, *117*
   fatal error, post-fight, 117–19
   Reputation Lock, breaking, 124–28
   Reputation Lock, costs of, *120*,
      120–24, *122*, *123*
   Reputation Lock, entering, 118–19,
      119
   Reputation Lock, inability to break,
      132–33
   stopping, 128–32, *131*, *132*
   toolbox, 134
Big Picture, *288*, 289
Birthday Fight, 83–112
   about, 84–86
   as circular fight, 96, *97*
   cycles, bad, 87–98
   Repairing Conversation and,
      99–110, *100*, *102–4*, *106–7*
   stopping, 98–110

   toolbox, 112
bombs, historical, 43, *43*
bridge, rebuilding, *290*, 290–91

caring, 139–44
   Defense Mode Actions, *143*,
      143–44, *144*
   loss of, *141*, 141–42
   threats and, 142–43, *143*
   ways of, *140*
   See also "You Don't Care About
      Me" Fight
changing, as avoidance tactic, 11
circular fights
   about, 34, *34*
   Birthday Fight as, 96, *97*
   defense/core tools for, 110–11
   Household Responsibilities Fight
      as, *66*, 66–67
Climate of Generosity, *73*, 73–75, *74*,
   78–81, *79*, *80*
Climate of Resentment, *72*, 72–73
closeness, 13, *13*, 15, *15*
Communication, Core-to-Core, *98*,
   98–99
complaints, 4, *5*
compromise, thinking beyond, 203–5
contributions, taking responsibility
   for, 35, 130
control, *239*, 239–40
core
   Bad Reputation Fight, 128, 130
   believing in, 128, 130
   Birthday Fight, 90

Defense Mode and, 116–17, *117*
defined, 292
Difficult Relatives Fight, 269, 270, 279, *279*
negative mindsets, stopping, 269, 270, 279, *279*
Repairing Conversation and, 101–3, *102–4*, 104, 105–6, *106–7*
speaking from your, 104, *104*
understanding your, 101–3, *102*, *103*
understanding your partner's, 105–6, *106*, *107*
Core Mode, 91, 292
Core-to-Core Communication, *98*, 98–99, 243–47, 294
criticism, 5, *5*
current arrows, 42, *42*
cycles, 37–38, 87–98
cyclical fights. *See* circular fights

Defense–Core Error
Bad Reputation Fight, 118, *118*
defined, 294
"You Don't Care About Me" Fight, *160*, 160–64, *162*, *163*
Defense Mode
Birthday Fight, 91–92, 98
core and, 116–17, *117*
defined, 292
Money Fight, 190–91
recognizing mutual, *99*, 99–100
Repairing Conversation, *99*, 99–100
Sex Fight, 228–29
threats and, 91–92, *92*
"You Don't Care About Me" Fight, 156–64, *158*, *159*, *160*, *162*, *163*
Defense Mode Actions
buildup of, 115–17, *117*
caring and, *143*, 143–44, *144*
defined, 293
as habits, 115

Repairing Conversation, 100, *100*, 101
stopping, committing to, 101
threats and, 93–96, *97*, 100, *100*
"You Don't Care About Me" Fight, *158*, 158–60, *159*
delight, *75*, 75–81, *76*
demands, 5, *5*
Difficult Relatives Fight, 255–83
about, 256–58
mindsets, negative, 263–68, *267*
stopping, by stopping negative mindsets, 268–83, *270–71*, *274–76*, *279*, *281–82*
stopping, difficulty of, 259–63, *260*, *261*, *262*
toolbox, 283
dissatisfaction, 222, *222–23*, 224–26
distance, 11–13, *12*, 14, *14*, 164
dreams, 188, *189*

empathy, 15, *15*, 206, *206–9*, 209–15
Escalating Fight, 39–53
about, 40–45, *42*, *43*, *44*
interrupting, 47–53, *49*, *50*, *52*
stopping, 45–46
toolbox, 53
expectations, *71*, 71–75

fears, 188, *189*
feedback without judgment, *10*, 10–11
Fight of All Fights, 138–39
"fire extinguisher" (fight-stopping reminder), 49–50, *50*
frequency of sex fights. *See* Sex Fight

generosity
appreciation and, *74*, 74–75
climate of, *73*, 73–75, *74*, 78–81, *79*, *80*
expectation and, *71*, 71–72

habits, 115
historical bombs, 43, *43*

history
emotional, 206, *206–9*, 209–15
negative mindsets, stopping, 269, 271
solving fights using, 216–19
Household Responsibilities Fight, 55–82
about, 56–67
as circular fight, *66*, 66–67
delight, opportunity to, 75–81
intent versus impact, 62, *62*
obligations and expectations, 67–75, *71*, *72*, *73*, *74*, *79*, *80*
toolbox, 82
hurt, expressing, 51–53, *52*

impact versus intent
Household Responsibilities Fight, 62, *62*
Nagging-Tuning Out Fight, 36–37
Proving Your Point Fight, *24*, 24–27, *25*, *26*, *27*
"You Don't Care About Me" Fight, *145*, 149–50
"I" statements, 10

judgment
feedback without, *10*, 10–11
Nagging-Tuning Out Fight, 35–36
Partner Improvement Fight, 8–11, *10*
removing, 8–10
Sex Fight, 225–29

kind requests, 4–5, *5*

learner-teacher relationship, 11–13, *12*
linear fights, 34
listening, selective, 178, *179*, 180
Little Picture, *287*, 287–88, 289

mindsets
changing, 247–52, 277–80, *281*, 282, *282*

negative, 263–68, *267*
partner's dilemma, 269–74, *270*, *271*
polarized, 260–62, *261*
resolving polarized, 274, 274–83, *275*, *276*, *279*, *281*, *282*
misinterpretation, *145*, 146–49
Money Fight, 187–220
about, 188–91
Defense Mode and, 190–91
dreams and fears, 188, *189*
history for solving, 216–19
as polarized fight, 192–201
stopping, 201–6, *206–9*, 209–15
toolbox, 220
mother-in-law, difficult. *See* Difficult Relatives Fight

Nagging-Tuning Out Fight, 29–38
about, 30–34
stopping, 35–38
toolbox, 38

"ouch," saying, 51–53, *52*

Pain Pictures, *287*, 287–88, 289
Parenting Differences Fight, 167–85
about, 168–74
as polarized fight, *174*, 174–80, *175*, *177*, *178*, *179*
stopping, 180–84, *181*, *182*, *183*
toolbox, 185
partner
core, understanding, 105–6, *106*, *107*
dilemma of, 269–74, *270*, *271*
focusing on, 15, *15*
See also specific topics
Partner Improvement Fight, 1–16
about, 2–8
advice, 11–15, *12*, *14*
changing to avoid, 11
judgment, feedback without, *10*, 10–11

judgment, removing, 8–10
Sex Fight and, 226–27
stopping, 8–10
toolbox, 16
polarized fights
  about, *174*, 174–75, *175*
  coming back from, 203
  compromise, thinking beyond,
    203–5
  emotional history and empathy,
    206, *206–9*, 209–15
  listening, selective, 178, *179*, 180
  Money Fight as, 192–201
  problem, agreeing on, 202
  reasoning, one-sided, 176–77, *177*,
    199–201
  solutions, opposing, 178, *178*,
    199–201
  stopping, 201–6, *206–9*, 209–15
  values, limiting to one, 176, 198
  values, outrage at ignored, *177*,
    177–78, 199–201
  values, reclaiming both, 180–84,
    181, *182*, *183*
problem
  agreeing on, 202
  different perspectives on, 259–60,
    260
  focusing on, 14, *14*
Proving Your Point Fight, 17–28
  about, 18–22
  stopping, 22–27, *24*, *25*, *26*, *27*
  toolbox, 28

questions, asking, 10

reasoning, one-sided, 176–77, *177*,
  199–201
Repairing Conversation, 99–110
  awareness, acting with, 107–10
  core, speaking from your, 104, *104*
  core, understanding your, 101–3,
    102, *103*

core, understanding your partner's,
  105–6, *106*, *107*
  Defense Mode, recognizing
    mutual, *99*, 99–100
  Defense Mode Actions,
    committing to stopping, 101
  Defense Mode Actions,
    recognizing threats caused by,
    100, *100*
Reputation Lock
  breaking, 124–28, *154*, 154–55, *155*
  breaking, difficulty of, 132–33
  costs of, *120*, 120–24, *122*, *123*
  defined, 294
  Difficult Relatives Fight, *262*,
    262–63
  entering, 118–19, *119*
  "You Don't Care About Me" Fight,
    154, 154–55, *155*
  See also Bad Reputation Fight
requests, 4–5, *5*
resentment, *72*, 72–73
Right–Wrong Fight. *See* Proving Your
  Point Fight

selective listening, 178, *179*, 180
Sex Fight, 221–53
  assumptions and, 225–26, 235–40,
    236–37, *239*
  control as issue, *239*, 239–40
  Defense Mode and, 228–29
  dissatisfaction and, 222, *222–23*,
    224–26
  judgment and, 225–29
  mindset, changing your, 247–52
  mismatch, about, 235–40, *236–37*,
    239
  mismatch, talking about, 243–47
  mismatch, using to spice things up,
    241, *241–43*, 243
  Partner Improvement Fight and,
    226–27
  toolbox, 253

solutions, opposing, 178, *178*, 199–201
spender/saver fights. *See* Money Fight
stuck, getting, 21
suggestions, 4–5, *5*

teacher-learner relationship, 11–13,
   12
terms used in this book, 292–94
thoughts, 125–26
threats
   Bad Reputation Fight, 130, *131*,
      132, *132*
   caring and, 142–43, *143*
   Defense Mode Actions and, 93–96,
      97, 100, *100*
   Defense Mode and, 91–92, *92*
   defined, 293
   Difficult Relatives Fight, 270, *270*,
      271, 271–72, 278
   finding, 130, *131*, 132, *132*
   negative mindsets, stopping, 270,
      270, *271*, 271–72, 278
   as Partner Improvement tool, 4–5, *5*
time-out, 48–50, *49*, *50*

values
   negative mindsets, stopping, *274*,
      274–76, *275*, *276*
   outrage at ignored, *177*, 177–78,
      199–201
   reclaiming both, 180–84, *181*, *182*,
      182–84, *183*
vulnerabilities, 269, 271

Weapons of Mass Destruction, 44, *44*,
   45

"You Don't Care About Me" Fight,
   135–65
   about, 136–38
   caring, 139–44, *140*, *141*, *143*, *144*
   Defense Mode and, 156–64, *158*,
      159, *160*, *162*, *163*

distance, bridging, 164
as Fight of All Fights, 138–39
stopping, *145*, 145–55, *154*, *155*
toolbox, 165

ABOUT THE AUTHOR

 **MICHELLE BRODY, PHD,** is an executive coach and clinical psychologist with over twenty years of experience as a practicing therapist and a specialist in resolving relational conflict. Her background also includes experience in teaching, coaching, and scientific research. She has served for more than a decade as a senior trainer for psychologists and a business consultant, teaching others how to catalyze lasting change. Dr. Brody is the founder of Coaching for Couples, an innovative practice for couples seeking time-efficient relationship change.